THE BALKARS
of SOUTHERN RUSSIA
and Their Deportation (1944–57)

www.hiddenpeoplesoftheworld.org

In all my travels around the world there has never been an experience quite like sitting in the home of a Balkar family, enjoying a meal in the midst of the breathtaking North Caucasus Mountains. This book will give you a greater glimpse of how the deportation of 1944 and attempted repatriation of 1957 have so drastically affected the lives of the Balkar people in the past and present. You will also learn much about their rich cultural heritage and how it impacts their everyday life. I highly recommend this book for anyone who desires to learn more about the neglected peoples of the North Caucasus.

Jonathan Grooms
president, Global Partners in Peace and Development
Blue Ridge, Virginia

I am deeply impressed with both the depth of Karen's research and her love for this tiny people group. The Balkars have suffered greatly in the last century, and they desperately need the peace of God in their hearts. It is my hope that this book will contribute to the growth of general awareness of the Caucasus peoples by the Western audience, and to more active involvement in promoting the work of the Gospel in this unstable and unreached part of the world.

Andrey Kravtsev
rector, North Caucasus Bible Institute
Prokhladny, Kabardino-Balkaria Republic, Russia

Karen has blended her personal experience with groundbreaking research of the Balkarians. This volume is a "must read" for both those studying the social dynamics of people movements and anyone wanting a better grasp of the folk ways and mores and devastation of a victimized and deported people group.

David Slamp, DMin
pastor, First Church of the Nazarene
Medford, Oregon

This book should be launched from the peaks of the highest European mountain, Mt. Elbrus, in Kabardino-Balkaria, so that the 1.4 billion English-speaking inhabitants of the world could hear the true information about the NKVD's (KGB) bloody actions upon the Balkar people nearly seventy years ago. Better late than never! This is a striking work which is and will be forever an unexpected recognition to the memory of those thousands of innocent victims of the Stalin-Beria genocide.

Boris Ulakov
English teacher among Balkarians
worker of the People's Education of the Russian Federation
teacher-methodologist, Köndelen, Kabardino-Balkaria Republic, Russia

THE BALKARS
of SOUTHERN RUSSIA
and Their Deportation (1944–57)

Karen Baker

WILLIAM CAREY
LIBRARY

Published by William Carey Library
1605 E. Elizabeth Street
Pasadena, CA 91104 | www.missionbooks.org

Melissa Hicks, editor
Brad Koenig, copyeditor
Amanda Valloza, graphic design
Rose Lee-Norman, indexer

William Carey Library is a ministry of the
U.S. Center for World Mission
Pasadena, CA | www.uscwm.org

Printed in the United States of America
17 16 15 14 13   5 4 3 2 1 BP300

Library of Congress Cataloging-in-Publication Data
Baker, Karen, 1948-
  The Balkars of Southern Russia and their deportation (1944-57) / Karen Baker.
    pages cm
  Includes bibliographical references.
  ISBN 978-0-87808-627-6
  1. Karachay (Turkic people)--History. 2. Forced migration--Soviet Union--History.
  3. Deportation--Soviet Union--History. 4. World War, 1939-1945--Soviet Union.
  I. Title.
  DK34.K26B367 2013
  947'.004943--dc23
                        2013015374

Dedicated to Verne Baker
My beloved husband, best friend,
and partner in our friendship with the Balkars.

In Memory of Zukhra Baysieva
A second generation Balkar, a sweet young woman
who served us *hichini* as we interviewed her father, Kaplan Baysiev,
and who died during the writing of this book.

Other book in the *Hidden Peoples of the World* series by the author:

Hidden Peoples of the World: The Mandaeans of Iraq, Saarbrücken, Germany, VDM Verlag Dr. Müller Aktiengesellschaft & Co. KG, 2009.

Global Partners in Peace and Development (GPPD)

Author proceeds from this book will be donated to Global Partners in Peace and Development to minister among the peoples of the North Caucasus region of Russia.

Contents

Photos

Note: All photos taken by author unless otherwise noted.

Tables

Maps

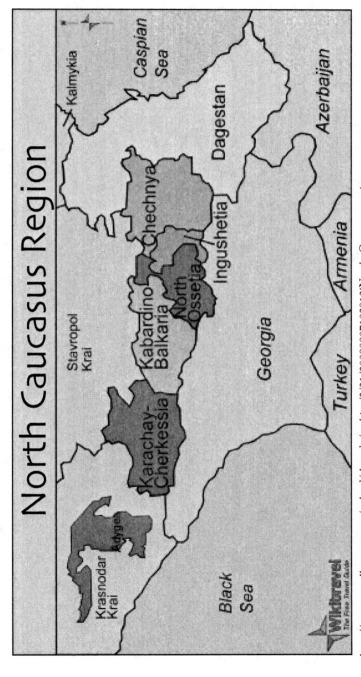

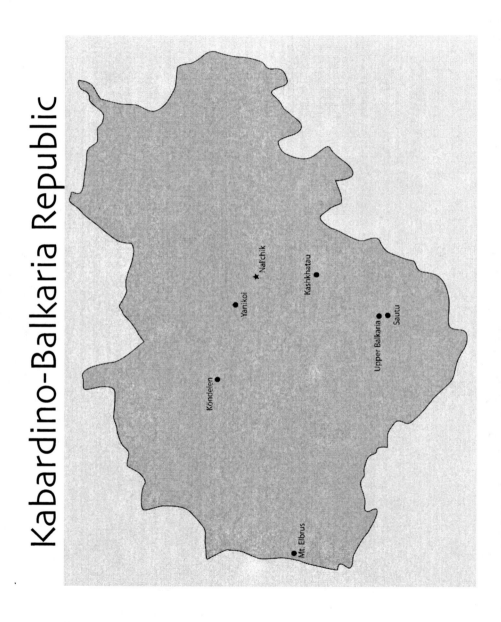

Kabardino-Balkaria Republic

Nalchik

Kashkhatau

Yanikol

Upper Balkaria

Sautu

Köndelen

Mt. Elbrus

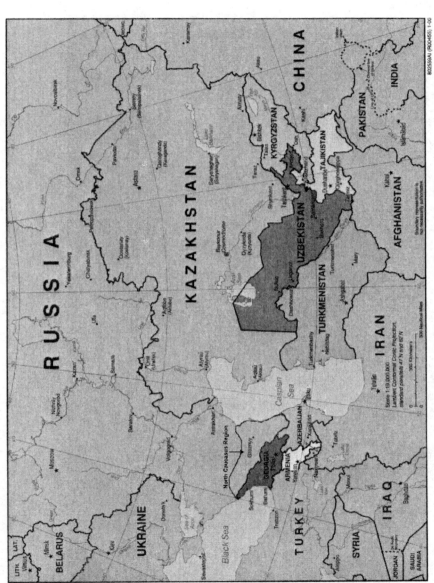

http://www.zonu.com/images/0X0/2009-09-17-583/Caucasus-and-Central-Asia-Political-Map-2000.jpg

Preface

Indelible events are often stamped into the consciousness of a nation. These events shape individuals, and often entire societies, in the way they view social, cultural, spiritual, political, and ethical realities. For my parents' generation, the Great Depression, followed by the Japanese attack on Pearl Harbor, shaped their outlook on money, conservation of resources, stability, the fragility of families, and their work ethic. In my generation, the assassination of President John F. Kennedy, the freedom of the 1960s, and the controversy of the Vietnam War created new rules and new priorities. For my daughter's generation, September 11, 2001, continues to plague their memories and has formed new realities as the quest for security has preempted personal privacy.

For Ibrahim Gelastanov, tears and emotion flooded his conversation about the deportation years. He cried as he recalled the details of his mother's death within twenty-four hours of arriving in a special settlement where she died of starvation. The topic of the deportation of 1944 is ever present in his conversation. From the moment I met him, he began to recount the horrors of his capture, the fifteen-day train ride, the forty-eight-hour boat ride, the twenty-four-hour walk to an unknown destination, and the starvation and indignities that he suffered. But Ibrahim always attributes his deportation as the means to his salvation into God's family. He was the first Balkarian Christian, and he remained the lone Balkar Christian for thirty-six years.

The tiny region of Balkaria is tucked into the largest mountain range of Europe, the Caucasus Mountains, in southern Russia. The Balkarians live in the shadow of unthinkable cruelty by the Stalin regime, the deportation of their entire people group. The deportation was concealed until the late twentieth century due to the secrecy of communism. It was also hidden behind the terrors that occurred in Europe during World War II. This book looks at the historical environment and facts of the deportation. Interviews with people who shared their vivid memories of the deportation, and with their descendants who continue to experience the repercussions of the deportation, augment the stark realities of this atrocity.

Acknowledgments

A book never involves only the author. There are many who have supported this work tangibly and intangibly, with help, advice, prayers, encouragement, and technical support. Only the dearest of friends do these things so willingly, and I thank each of you. I especially thank my brother-in-law, Robert Johnson, who graciously edited all the photos to publication standards.

My deepest gratitude goes to the Balkars themselves who shared their stories so readily, and for those who enabled that effort by driving, introducing me to people, interpreting the language, and interpreting the culture. Ultimately, all credit goes to the Author of everything, my Lord and Savior Jesus Christ, who put the idea into motion and who provided the means to travel, the health to pursue the stories, the resources for the research, and the affirmations at many milestones.

Abstract

The deportation of entire ethnic groups of the North Caucasus region of southern Russia was an immense operation of the Soviet government during World War II. Entire people groups[1], called nations or nationalities, were exiled to other places in the Soviet Union based on perceived behaviors of a few individuals. They endured hardship, death, starvation, and personal indignities during weeks-long train rides for thousands of miles in cattle cars. Once deposited at their destinations, they were placed at additional risk of death due to climate, working conditions, disease, and famine.

The Balkarians, or Balkars,[2] were forcibly taken from their native homelands and deported to distant lands within the Soviet Union. They remained in exile for thirteen years. The third generation of Balkars since that horrible experience continues to live in the shadow of the atrocities committed against their people. This book applies comprehensive research to the facts of the deportation. More importantly, it examines lingering resentments and current sentiments of the Balkarians through extensive personal interviews with those who experienced the deportation and with their descendants.

---

1   A group of people who are related ethnically, linguistically, culturally, traditionally, and geographically. This book uses people group, ethnic group, nation, and nationality interchangeably.

2   The people of this ethnicity refer to themselves using the terms Balkar and Balkarian interchangeably. Thus, the author has preserved this intermingling of terms throughout this book.

Introduction

Often events impacting a nation go beyond a generation. The deportation of the Armenian population by the Ottoman Empire, and the resultant massacres, starvation, and death from exposure continue to haunt Armenian survivors and their descendants. The effects of the genocide of Armenians from 1915 to 1919 is an ever-present reality, as permanent refugees look from their slum apartments toward Mount Ararat and are reminded of those they lost—siblings, parents, and children.

Refugees from Iraq bitterly show the scars which were inflicted by the hands of Saddam Hussein's forces in the last half of the twentieth century. We continue to see the effect of these memories as they flee to countries around the world to start their lives over.

The greatest impact of the twentieth century is the Holocaust. "The genocide of 6 million European Jews was a unique event in both scope and kind, but it was also the most extreme manifestation of the contemporary practice of ethnic cleansing."[3] The creation of a homeland for a nation that had been dispersed around the world for nearly two thousand years is a monumental testament to God's faithfulness to His Word, as Israel continues to be in the headlines sixty years after its creation.

The deportation of entire nations by their mother country is an untold story that lies below the radar of the tragedies of World War II, or the Great Patriotic War as it was called in the Soviet Union. Over 12 million Soviet soldiers were killed in this war. Many were from the nations, or nationalities, within the USSR who were punished, along with their families, by the very government they were serving. While several nationalities throughout the USSR faced similar circumstances, this book focuses on the smallest of these nations, Balkaria, with a population estimated at less than fifty thousand at the time of the deportation in March 1944. It is estimated that 25 percent of those deported died either in the transport or the struggle of adapting to a new environment due to hunger, disease, climate, and frailty. The Soviet Union, and its predecessor, the Russian Empire, carried out deportations, or population realignments, throughout history. This, however, was the only time in which entire people groups were targeted based solely on their ethnicity. This book analyzes not only the events of that time, but the lingering effects of the deportation on successive generations.

---

3   Terry Martin, "The Origins of Soviet Ethnic Cleansing," *Journal of Modern History* 70 (December 1998): 819.

The North Caucasus region is a six-hundred-mile-wide mountainous strip of land located in southern Russia between the Black Sea and the Caspian Sea. This land is home to over fifty different people groups, or nations, each with their own language, culture, and geographical territory. These fifty-plus peoples live in seven of the eighty-nine subjects (internal provinces) of the Russian Federation, and the inhabitants are citizens of Russia. The Balkarians are a tiny nationality in this Caucasus region of Russia, and live primarily in the Kabardino-Balkaria Republic (KBR).

The cruelty inflicted by the Stalin regime during World War II against its own citizens has made an indelible mark on the consciousness of the people of this tiny nation. The atrocities that were committed within the USSR have gone unnoticed for decades due to the secrecy and control of information by the Soviet government. The relative lack of attention throughout the Cold War era by scholars in the West towards the non-Russian nationalities of the USSR is explained by the inability to gain access to archives in Moscow, St. Petersburg, or in the local nations. Keeping the secrets of the Stalin era was

the consequence of seeing the Soviet Union through the lens of the Cold War. As the Soviet Union and the United States became embroiled in conflicts across the globe, Western observers became accustomed to thinking about "the Soviets" as an undifferentiated whole, and as the polar opposite of "the Americans."[4]

This inaccessibility of archival information prevented serious research prior to 1989. The first academic work on the deportations was published by Russian scholar Aleksandr Nekrich, doctor of historical sciences at the Institute of History of the Soviet Academy of Sciences, after he was forced to leave his country in the 1970s for attempting to publish the history of the deported peoples.

In 1989 Soviet President Mikhail Gorbachev instituted policies which opened the archives and exposed the Soviet Union's past behaviors to the world. As this small stream of information began flowing to the outside world, researchers were enabled to probe into the internal actions of the Stalin years.

The Soviet Union began breaking up as nationalities within it demanded their independence in the early 1990s. The Bolsheviks had only secured these borders in the 1920s, so it is essential to look at the policies that governed these nations in the early twentieth century.

In my visit to this region in 2008, the first Balkarian man I met, Ibrahim Gelastanov, shared his story of the deportation of 1944 within minutes of

---

4   Francine Hirsch, *Empire of Nations* (New York: Cornell University Press, 2005), 2.

our introduction. I felt multiple emotions of shock, outrage, sympathy, and astonishment. I had never heard such things before. As I researched and interviewed those who had experienced the deportation of the Balkarians, I became more stunned and more ashamed that such things had happened and the world was unaware of them. Even within Russia these facts are still unknown or misunderstood because of the official misinformation the government has perpetrated. The world goes on about its business without awareness of these offenses that have been borne in silence and isolation by the Balkars. Recognizing that the words shared by those who experienced the deportation tell us more about their present-day state of mind than the specifics of the experience, the story must be told within its historical context, and the impact on the people of this little nation must be examined.

1
The Cultural History and Traditions of the Balkarians

Russia is the largest country in the world with over 17 million square miles. It is nearly twice the size of the United States. It spans two continents, Europe and Asia, and nine time zones. It borders fifteen foreign nations. Russia's population of over 143 million is the ninth largest in the world and boasts a literacy rate of over 99 percent. There are over 160 different ethnic groups with over one hundred languages spoken in Russia. Approximately fifty of these different languages are spoken in the North Caucasus alone, one of the greatest diversities of languages in a region of this size anywhere on the planet.

Scholars have tried to look at this region geographically, linguistically, and historically, and they have ultimately come to the conclusion that it is unique. The variety of topography and climate helps account for the multiplicity of political, cultural, and economic influences that have long defined the region. Ancient Roman writers claimed that scores of translators were required when traders sought to do business there. Arab geographers labeled the region the "mountain of languages." "According to the tenth-century Arab scholar al-Masudi, the peoples who lived there could only be numbered by Him who made them . . . The Caucasian mountaineers as a whole are made up of fragments of almost every race and people in Europe and Western Asia."[5] The ethnic diversity on this narrow slice of land lying between two major Eurasian seas has meant that the range of disparate cultures has been even more extreme than in most places and has been bound together by its geographic isolation. The diversity of languages, religious practices, and social structures throughout the entire North Caucasus region is squeezed into a territory approximately the size of Florida.

Identifying and defining the peoples of the North Caucasus region of southern Russia is not an easy task. It has been labeled the "museum of nations" because this mountainous strip of land wedged between the Black Sea and the Caspian Sea has more nationality borders per square mile than any other on earth. There are an estimated forty-five to fifty nationalities indigenous to this region. Each of these people groups possesses their

---

5   Charles King, *The Ghost of Freedom: A History of the Caucasus* (New York: Oxford University Press, 2008), 9.

own language, history, and culture. The Balkarian people are a part of the Kabardino-Balkaria Republic (KBR), one of seven republics in the North Caucasus mountain region. Kabardino-Balkaria is roughly the size of the state of Connecticut.

> The mountains themselves had belonged to no empire: they may have been coloured in on generals' charts, but throughout these generations, myriad cultures survived ... [By the 1820s they were] an undefeated people, their independence and ethics very much intact.[6]

It took the Russian tsars more than two hundred years to conquer the Caucasus region, an endeavor that began at the end of the sixteenth century against the Ottoman and Persian Empires. The peoples of the Caucasus fought fiercely for their freedom from Russian aggression.

> They did not realize the tremendous odds they were facing. They were too remote from the world of political and diplomatic realities of the nineteenth century to understand either the hopelessness of their own situation or the power of the Russian Empire.[7]

By 1864 the Caucasus wars had come to an end. The valiant efforts of the Caucasus peoples were crushed. By the mid-1800s the school system of the Caucasus was "fully incorporated into the Russian imperial network, with graduates of Caucasus schools regularly going on to Russian universities. Libraries, museums and scholarly societies were also set up."[8] The educational system concentrated specifically on substituting the Russian language for the local ethnic languages.

Photos 1 & 2: A fort and towers from ancient times still stand.

---

6   Nicholas Griffin, *Caucasus: A Journey to the Land between Christianity and Islam* (Chicago: University of Chicago Press, 2001), 45.

7   Walter Kolarz, *Russia and Her Colonies* (New York: Praeger, 1952), 181.

8   King, *Ghost of Freedom*, 86.

However, the powerful military of the Russian Empire could not subdue these nations easily. Resistance and uprisings were the norm for the following sixty years. The peoples of the North Caucasus fought for the "most basic liberty: not to answer to a foreigner."[9] For decades after the Russian conquest, the nations of the Caucasus "continued to be a source of uneasiness to the Russian state. Complete Russian victory over the rebellious mountaineers was achieved only under the Soviet regime."[10]

The Tsarist Empire of Russia collapsed after World War I. Vladimir Lenin and the Bolsheviks carried out a coup in 1917 and forced the country into the grip of Bolshevik communism under the title of the Union of Soviet Socialist Republics (USSR). It was finally in 1920 that the Soviet Union could claim sovereignty over the North Caucasus region as the Bolsheviks crushed the final resistance of the mountain peoples. "This Soviet system was based on deception, intimidation, and force. Manipulation of various forms of terror and threat of terror became the dominant characteristic of the Soviet art of governing."[11]

Photo 3: Horses run wild in the mountains.

As early as the 1600s, the Muscovites' method of dealing with the Caucasus peoples involved the threat of capture. It was common practice in this part of the world to engage in kidnapping, or taking captives, in order to exact ransoms for their return. The enterprise of kidnapping hostages and requiring ransoms between nations, as well as between individuals, became a form of adoption into the conquering culture. For those peoples who were always at war, there was little time for peaceful labor. Those who were not farmers had no means of providing for

---

9   Yoʻav Karny, *Highlanders: A Journey to the Caucasus in Quest of Memory* (New York: Farrar, Straus & Giroux, 2000), xiv.

10   Kolarz, *Russia and Her Colonies*, 182.

11   Paul B. Henze, "Russia and the Caucasus," Circassian World, accessed February 20, 2010, http://www.circassianworld.com/new/north-caucasus/1176-russia-and-the-caucasus-henze.html,

themselves, and so the kidnapping was a justified economic endeavor. In return for kidnapped individuals, particularly Russian military and wealthy men, handsome ransoms provided sustenance for the highlanders, the name commonly applied to these mountain peoples. Thus, "when Russia approached the Caucasus, there had already been a long history of interaction with indigenous peoples over the issue of captive-taking."[12]

Ethnology is the study of various peoples and the differences and relationships among them, as well as the historical development of culture among peoples. When speaking of relatedness among the peoples of the North Caucasus, the relationship is nearly always measured in terms of native languages. There are many theories as to how so many languages ended up in such a small geographic area. Some of the world's greatest armies have invaded the land or used it as a base to conquer even further lands. Alexander the Great, who allegedly used the Caucasus as the dumping ground for exiled criminals and undesirables, is said to have counted three hundred separate languages in the Caucasus. The Persians invaded the mountains many times, as did the Turkish, Mongol, Armenian, and Russian Empires. Germans colonized it. Christianity took root among the Ossetian people, bringing bits of Latin to this land. "Languages were wholly separate . . . as speakers of mutually unintelligible languages might be separated by only a mountain or river."[13] The most likely

> explanation for the diversity of languages is that the impassable terrain and harsh climate kept small communities free from external influence . . . [Since] no centralizing cultural influence forced the fragments together . . . [these languages] remained in their pristine state—unwritten, unread, and helpfully uncontested.[14]

There are four primary linguistic groups in the North Caucasus. The Turkic group includes the Balkarians and their relatives, the Karachay people. The Turkic peoples, and several of the peoples of the eastern Caucasus, historically resisted Russian authority the longest and most vigorously, while other North Caucasus peoples more willingly submitted to the Russians. Some attribute this past rebelliousness to the deportation of the Turkic peoples, the Karachay and Balkarians.

A social inventory of the Caucasus was completed as part of the first comprehensive imperial census in 1897. The "Caucasus was seen to be peopled by clearly delineated religious and linguistic groups . . . The universal

---

12   King, *Ghost of Freedom*, 53.
13   Ibid., 36.
14   Karny, *Highlanders*, xvi.

category of 'highlander' had disappeared, replaced by an array of terms that closely mapped modern ethnic categories."[15] Though these ethnicities had not yet taken on the significance that they acquired in the 1920s, it is noteworthy that the census showed the vast array of groups which populated the North Caucasus region. The arbitrary ethnic designations came when Russia invaded the Caucasus during the late eighteenth century. Names "were often forced onto the natives through historical ignorance and a lack of common sense."[16]

Photo 4: The traditional Balkarian costumes are ornate and beautiful.

"Elements of Balkar culture indicate a long association with the Near East, the Mediterranean, the rest of the Caucasus, and Russia."[17] Over the course of centuries, foreign invaders drove the Balkars higher into the Caucasus Mountains, into the alpine meadows and torrent valleys, just below the mountain glaciers. Eighty-seven percent of the population lived in rural areas. They lived mainly by animal husbandry, raising sheep, goats, cattle, horses, and donkeys; hunting; orchard farming; and beekeeping. Their diet consisted of all types of meat that they raised, as well as vegetables and dairy products. Traditional Balkar foods included sour boiled milk, called *ayran,* and *kefir,* a type of liquid yogurt. The women, in addition to being excellent cooks, had a reputation for their sewing and textile skills: they spun wool, made cloth, and created the large pieces of felt for which they are legendary. Their artistic applique work is a part of the traditional dress of the Balkars.

"Little is known of the daily lives of the inhabitants of the Caucasus until modern times. But one thing that is certain is the fact that their identities were always relational."[18] The Balkars had customs, called *adats,* which regulated social and moral behavior. These traditions defined personal

15   King, *Ghost of Freedom,* 144.
16   Karny, *Highlanders,* xvii.
17   Ibragim Shamanov and Paul Friedrich, "Balkars," Encyclopedia.com, accessed November 13, 2009, http://www.encyclopedia.com.
18   King, *Ghost of Freedom,* 15.

behavior, lifestyle, gender roles, and respect and veneration for elders. These customs regulated hospitality to guests, military valor, bravery, honesty, honor, loyalty, and tolerance. These rules were passed on orally, kept order in the community, and are still revered.

Even today,

> no asphalt roads were to be found, and local transportation was confined to a few tractors and horse-drawn carts. Families shared their fenced yards with domestic animals, and at the outskirts of the village were poorly dressed, wet-nosed kids—all-too-familiar representatives of rural poverty worldwide.[19]

Photo 5: Village road in Upper Balkaria.

Cows meandered freely throughout the villages, often taking the road and blocking any horse-drawn carts or the few cars that ventured there.

Toma Kulbaeva grew up in the city of Nalchik, but often visited her grandmother in one of the villages. She described her perspective on village life:

> Villages are usually small. In my grandmother's village, there are only sixty houses. There is one shop in the village, one first-aid post, one veterinary surgeon, who is my cousin. If someone has a sick cow, my cousin goes to him. If a person is ill, it is necessary to drive him to the city; it is 80 kilometers [approximately 50 miles] and the roads are very bad.

Photo 6: Boys on a milk truck in Balkarian village.

19   Karny, *Highlanders*, 353.

People live in poverty in the village. To survive, it is necessary to work hard. There are only a few jobs, and going to the city is too distant. In the first-aid post, there are two workers; one is my aunt and the other is a driver. There is one woman who works in the shop. And my cousin is the veterinary surgeon. And that's all. There are no jobs anymore. Many people drink [alcohol] because of unemployment, in all of the Balkarian villages.

The school for the children is in the next village. The bus picks the children up and takes them home. Many of the Balkar children do not speak Russian very well.

People try to have some cows. Cows provide milk, and then it is possible to make cheese, sour cream, cottage cheese, butter, and yogurt. But it is very difficult to look after cattle, and not everyone can do the hard work required. The people who have cattle have no time to rest, especially in the summer with haymaking. Both men and women take part in it. My cousins work with their father on their own land. They are ten and fourteen years old. They are already used to the hard work, and they work as hard as their father. All families make their own bread.

Most homes have water, but not hot water. Most homes do not have toilets or bathing. They heat water and use a large tub to bathe. My aunt's family is the first in her village to have a bathtub and hot water. My cousin constructed everything, because he hopes to have tourists from Moscow, St. Petersburg, and Rostov stay at their home when they come to the mountains for holiday, since there are no hotels in the mountains. Now my cousin at least has work for the summer. Tourists come to fly on gliders.

Most homes have electricity. They have internet and television. It's absurd: some people don't have hot water, but they have the Internet!

There are still a few of the adobe homes, burrowed into the mountainside. My grandmother's house still stands as she will not allow anyone to tear it down. Now a newer house is built near her old one, which is where the family lives now.

Photo 7: The adobe house of Toma's grandmother remains burrowed into the mountainside.

Despite all these difficulties, to live in the village is safer than in the city. Every day there are acts of terrorism, gunshots in the city. Some people accuse the police. Some people accuse Islamists. Many parents began to forbid their children from going to the mosque. Many continue to believe that having killed non-Muslims they will go to paradise. For example, one family lost their son and daughter who were in hiding a very long time because of the terrorism. They are assured that they are in paradise because they killed non-believers [in Islam].

Many parents think it is better for their children to drink and smoke, rather than follow Jesus. I do not know how many addicts and alcoholics there are in our republic, but I know there are many. My father met one man, a Chechen, who was an addict for years. Now this man works with my father to take addicts to a Christian rehabilitation center.

The crime is growing in my republic. First, there is a lot of corruption. Even the worst pupil can have excellent grades if his parents bribe the teacher. Any student can get good marks without going to class. Any person can find good work if they pay money to get the job. Even if you are better in your profession than others, if you do not have the money, you should wait for a miracle. But we believers in Christ know that only God can help, rather than money.[20]

Caucasian ethnicity is often used as a synonym for "white" in American culture. However, its true meaning refers to the "indigenous inhabitants of the Caucasus, some of whom are white or pale, some swarthy, some dark."[21] The use of the word "Caucasian" to identify race was developed around 1800 by a German scientist, Johann Friedrich Blumenbach, based on his analysis of physical traits and the head size of people from the South Caucasus Mountains. This word is commonly used in America to identify "race," but that is truly a misuse of the term. In this book, "Caucasian" refers to people whose ethnic identity is derived from the geographical location of the Caucasus Mountains.

At the turn of the century, about 35 percent of the North Caucasus population of 9 million was Sunni Muslim, with the remainder divided between various strains of Christianity (including Russian and Georgian Orthodox, Armenian Gregorian, Armenian Catholic, Roman Catholic, and German Lutheran), Judaism, and Buddhism.[22] There are elements of traditional animist and pagan worship which preceded the entrance of Christianity and Islam. Furthermore, the distinctions between Christians and Muslims are often blurred as holidays and rituals are very similar for all peoples, regardless of religion, and have clear roots in history. In fact, among the inhabitants of the mountains is a Jewish and quasi-Jewish community who trace their origins to the destruction of the first Jewish temple in 586 BC, when the Israelites were deported from Jerusalem by the Babylonians (present-day Iraq) and subsequently came under the rule of the Persians

---

20   Toma Kulbaeva, interview by author, October 2, 2010, Moneta, Virginia, transcript.
21   Karny, *Highlanders*, xvi.
22   King, *Ghost of Freedom*, 145.

(present-day Iran). Throughout the region, there are reports of Muslims who light candles on Fridays and can be seen carrying fragments from the Torah scrolls. People of both Christian and Muslim faith "enjoyed alcohol, were far removed from clerical authority and practiced a form of folk religion that bore only scant resemblance to the orthodox varieties found elsewhere."[23] Now, the majority of the population self-identify themselves as Sunni Muslim, even though the practice of Islam varies widely from the perceived norm. As will be discussed in detail, most Balkars are Muslim by tradition, not by practice.

In 1918 several of the North Caucasus nations formed the Mountain Republic. In 1920 the Soviet government designated the inhabitants of the North Caucasus into the Autonomous Mountain Socialist Soviet Republic. This republic included all of the North Caucasus peoples: the Kabardinians, Chechens, Dagestanis, Circassians (Cherkess), Ingush, Ossetians, Balkarians, and Karachay. The Soviets imposed registration by ethnicity, making ethnic awareness prominent.

It did not take long for the Soviet leaders to realize that uniting the mountain peoples could interfere with their plans to centralize the government. It was only twenty months later, in September 1921, that Lenin, through his newly appointed commissar of nationalities, Joseph Stalin, began the disintegration of the Mountain Republic. The Bolsheviks

consolidated control over the ethnically complex North Caucasus through classic divide-and-rule techniques. Peoples were allocated separate "autonomous" republics and regions, areas of mixed populations were shifted arbitrarily, and unrelated ethnic groups with few common interests were joined together so that each would serve to restrain tendencies toward self-assertion among the other . . . [This] ethnic structuralism proved to be a recipe for permanent tension in a region as ethnically diverse as the Caucasus.[24]

The Kabardinians were designated an autonomous province. A few months later the Balkars were officially joined with the Kabardinians in the newly named Kabardino-Balkaria Autonomous Province in 1922. To the west was created a separate autonomous province—Karachay-Cherkessia.

The delineation of political boundaries has long been a source of contention. For example, the Kabardinians and the Cherkess are ethnically related, and the Karachay and Balkars are ethnically related. By joining them with dissimilar if not antagonistic peoples, the Soviets sought to create tension, rather than unity, in order to forestall any future uprisings.

---

23   Ibid., 56.
24   Henze, "Russia and the Caucasus."

This placement, of course, also made them easier to control.

Where there had been one political entity across the North Caucasus region, "there were now seven ethnic republics, regions and districts, all nominally autonomous, giving the area more national borders per square mile than any other part of the world."[25] This region was also populated by large numbers of ethnic Russians, especially the industrial centers in the western part of the North Caucasus.

In 1936 the Kabardino-Balkar Autonomous Province was upgraded into the Kabardino-Balkar Autonomous Soviet Socialist Republic (ASSR). The population of the republic in 1939 was 349,700—43 percent Russian, 36.3 percent Kabardinians, and 11.1 percent (39,000) Balkarians.

This political maneuvering had, however, not dealt with the basic problem of assimilating the mountain peoples into "reliable Soviet citizens and how to associate them with the socialist transformation of society."[26] This became painfully obvious in 1942 when the Germans occupied much of the North Caucasus region during World War II. Over twenty years of Soviet rule had not altered the conviction of the mountain dwellers that the USSR's foes were their friends. Some of these peoples gave assistance to the German invaders.

> Of the seven peoples who in 1920 had formed the Mountain Republic, four had shown themselves particularly unreliable in the crucial winter of 1942–43 . . . [including] the Balkars (42,660) . . . After the North Caucasus region had been cleared of the invaders [the Germans], the Soviet Government found itself unable to forgive these nationalities for their disloyalty or even their indifference. It also abandoned all further attempts to transform them into good citizens of the USSR and expelled them from the "happy family of Soviet peoples."[27]

The Balkar nation (and several other North Caucasus nations) were deported in 1944 and remained in exile until 1957. Some of the autonomous provinces and republics were abolished. The Kabardinian-Balkarian ASSR was renamed the Kabardinian ASSR after having been relieved of the "burden" of the Balkar traitors. From 1944 until 1957, the Balkars were banished in public documents, as if they had never existed. The rewriting of history had begun.

In 1947 the official encyclopedia of the Soviet Union listed all of the peoples of the country with some astonishing omissions: there was no mention of the Balkars. It documented the ethnic composition of the Kabardin Republic in 1933 as 60 percent Kabardin and 10.7 percent Russian.

25   Karny, *Highlanders*, xviii.
26   Kolarz, *Russia and Her Colonies*, 183.
27   Ibid., 185.

"There was no explanation for why the figures did not add up to 100 percent . . . There was a chilling echo of their absence . . . They were still alive in exile, but they had ceased to exist as recognized entities."[28] Not only had the Balkars lost their homelands, but they had lost any public acknowledgment of their existence, past or present. The Balkars were erased from history by the USSR.

---

28   Oliver Bullough, *Let Our Fame Be Great* (New York: Basic Books, 2010), 210.

2
Clocks and Calendars

Photo 8: The table is set for guests.

The law of hospitality always prevails when guests arrive at the home of a Balkar family, regardless of whether their coming was expected. There is nothing on the calendar that supersedes the guests at the door. Time stops as all are welcomed as family, whether friends or strangers. "Children are scattered in all directions through the village and up the hill, sent with messages to brothers and cousins that a sheep will be roasted for the guests."[29] King appropriately describes their hospitality as "wildly extravagant."[30] Tea, of course, is the glue that holds the nation together. As soon as a guest enters the home, the women begin preparing food. The hot tea is served, followed by savory and/or sweet delicacies. This is not a mere snack, but rather a feast. It could include soup, bread, freshly made cheese, meats, meat- or vegetable-filled pastries, and cabbage rolls.

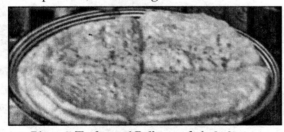

Photo 9: Traditional Balkarian dish, *hichini*, is prepared for guests.

The most famous traditional Balkarian food is *hichini*, a labor-intensive dish which is the centerpiece of any meal and the pride of every host. It is dough—made of flour, water, shredded potatoes, and onions—rolled very thin like a crepe. The *hichini* is then fried, one at a time. While still hot, each *hichini* is slathered with butter, and the *hichini* are stacked several inches high and eaten one at a time by hand.

29   Griffin, *Caucasus*, 39.
30   King, *Ghost of Freedom*, 105.

The food is prepared on the spot, even if a guest was not expected or unknown to the household. There is no such thing as stopping by for a brief visit; all visits last at least an hour, and the host is dishonored if the guests will not stay for the spread.

It is clearly the role of the women to prepare such treats. On one occasion, my friends and I were unscheduled and unknown, seeking an interview with a Balkar man who was recommended to us. We were warmly welcomed into the home by the man, his son, and his grandson. As he told his story, he continually apologized because the women were not home to prepare tea. Apparently neither the son nor the grandson was adequately acquainted with the kitchen in order to boil water for tea.

The Balkarian tradition of washing hands before meals requires a specific pitcher and basin used for the occasion. Since most of the village homes do not have indoor plumbing, the basin and pitcher are kept readily available. As modernity enters the Balkarian culture, most notably indoor plumbing in the cities, the use of these items is becoming unnecessary.

Photo 10: Author with Alim Kulbaev washing hands with traditional pitcher and basin.

Photo 11: An antique pitcher and basin used for handwashing.

Photo 12: The dances include the water pitcher, a symbol of Balkarian life.

Respect is a custom that is strictly adhered to.

The main thing in our culture is respect. This is like an unwritten constitution. If someone dies [all of the neighboring villages] send people to the funeral. It is the same for a wedding. We share happiness, we share sadness. And if someone is older than you, you respect him, even if he is only two or three years older.[31]

Respect for elders is a very strongly observed custom. Young people do not speak in the presence of their elders. Grown men will sit with guests in their home, but when their father is present, they say very little, even if spoken to directly. This custom was clearly observed in the above-mentioned home, where the son and grandson sat as silent witnesses to the conversation but did not participate.

Photo 13: Boris Ulakov in his office/library.

Boris Ulakov was the first English teacher among the Balkarians. He received many honors for his excellence as a teacher-methodologist in his field, and can point to many of his students who have achieved success due to their command of the English language. He is very proud of his heritage and spent hours with the author to communicate the details of the Balkarian traditions.

One is required to rise when someone passes on the road or when someone enters the home. You must never clean your nose in the presence of others; Russians can blow their nose in front of others, but Balkarians would never do that. When riding a horse, one must dismount as he passes the cemetery. Younger people never are seated in the presence of older people; they must stand up and offer their place to the elder person. I cannot drink in the presence of my older brother; I can never smoke in the company of my older brother.[32]

Even how parents relate to children is dictated by the law of respect. However, there are downsides to traditions. Boris, now a seventy-year-old man, expressed his distress as he shared his heartbreak of years gone by.

---

31   Bullough, *Fame*, 41.
32   Boris M. Ulakov, interview by author, March 22, 2011, Köndelen, Kabardino-Balkaria, tape recording and transcript.

His recollections were stated with such pain as if they had happened in the past week. He said:

> My mother was brought up so very deeply in the Balkar customs. She was not permitted to embrace me, or kiss me, even when I left for travel in other countries as a young man. My parents and grandparents lived in the same house and shared our yard with all the relatives. It was not allowed for her to say her sons' names in the presence of her mother-in-law or father-in-law. She only addressed me as "a son," not by name, not even by "my son." Even until her death, she did not use my name to address me. I tried not to care, but it still hurts very badly. She wouldn't even call my father by his name, but only "the owner of my head" or the "head of the household." She could not say his name.[33]

There is no thought of retirement in the Caucasus Mountains. Elders not only work but are also esteemed as the custodians of culture, expected to attend all the rites of life as well as to transfer their knowledge to the succeeding generations. This is aided by the customary role of the youngest (or only) son and his wife when he marries. The youngest son brings his wife to the family home, where they will raise their family and care for his aging parents. It is his obligation to take care of his parents until their deaths. According to the traditional law of inheritance, the youngest son eventually inherits the parents' home and property. This practice continues even to the first and second generations for those Caucasians who have emigrated to America. It provides a clear process of familial responsibilities. It is a predictable and practical method of not only who will inherit the family home and land, but also who will care for the elderly parents. Further, it keeps the parents connected with the family in a very respectful manner. There is never a question of who will take care of them.

Shame is the worst thing that can befall a family, and when one person within the family goes outside the boundaries of tradition, the entire family is dishonored. There are expectations of separating the sexes in virtually every circumstance, honoring persons who are older than oneself, appropriate dress (though this generally applies only to females rather than males), hygiene, etc. Though many of these cultural traditions seem to be loosening a bit, they are still a very strong boundary which is only breached very carefully. For example, women are expected to wear dresses all the time. In fact, there are "house dresses" which are a bit more casual and are worn only in the home. Younger women in the cities are departing from this rigid requirement slowly but, even for them, visits to the villages are only made when appropriately dressed (wearing a dress, not pants), as the villagers still have a more conservative

---

33   Ibid.

view of decorum. Women will often be seen wearing headscarves in public, especially in the villages. Newlywed young women are required to wear the scarves in the home as well, until the husband or mother-in-law determines that enough time has lapsed since the marriage to end this requirement. It is usually not more than a year.

3
Weddings and Funerals

Marriage customs are adhered to very strictly. "First cousins cannot marry; Balkarians never marry their relatives," Boris emphasized, as he continued to describe an array of Balkar traditions.[34] Balkars have traditionally been monogamous, even after Islam became the primary religion and allowed up to four wives. The *adat* strictly enforced endogamy, which is marriage within one's social class. And it would be unthinkable to marry outside of the nationality. Even today's young women express a preference to marry a Balkarian, regardless of any other consideration.

Photo 14: Madina Zhanataeva, a third-generation Balkarian.

Toma Kulbaeva is a young woman who was raised in a Christian Balkar family. For her, it would be preferable to marry a Balkar who was Muslim, rather than a non-Balkar Christian.[35] Madina Zhanataeva is a Muslim, but has an older sister who is a Christian. She too places the highest priority on marrying a Balkar. Religion is not a concern for her. She says, "If he was a Christian, I would hope to convert him to Islam. By marrying a Balkar, at least we have some things in common in our culture, and Islam does have some similarities to Christianity."[36]

Balkarian wedding traditions are similar to other Caucasus cultures with the "stolen" or "kidnapped" bride being a central element of the occasion. The marriages are not generally arranged by parents. If the parents do not know each other, the boy will never go to the girl's home until the wedding. Marrying well into the late twenties is not uncommon.

Kidnapping or bride stealing is still a major component of the Balkar culture. Bride stealing has roots at least as far back as the 1800s and was a

---

34   Ulakov, interview.

35   T. Kulbaeva, interview, 2010.

36   Madina Zhanataeva, interview by author, March 19, 2011, Nalchik, Kabardino-Balkaria, tape recording.

common practice among not only the highland mountain peoples, but also at various times by the Russians, Cossacks, Georgians, and others.[37]

> The kidnapping of a bride was not considered a crime, but a ritual, both families often content when the young [man] would gallop up to his intended, throw her over the saddle and disappear . . . [In today's Caucasian society, a father] reminisced how his son kidnapped his bride: "He took her from the street, put her in his car and drove away. It is like elopement, but being kidnapped is more romantic."[38]

In fact, bride stealing and raids taking hostages were both considered economic issues. There is great shame associated with either the family taking their daughter back, or with her refusal to go with the young man. In today's practice among the Balkars, the method of courtship is well established and well understood by the Balkarians of all ages. The young man always initiates the first contact and they meet in an open place, such as a café or a walk in a public park. The first date is considered the first step toward marriage. It is up to the boy to broach the subject of marriage with the girl. It would be very unlikely that the girl would ever initiate such a discussion, even among close friends or family. All of their dates must be in public places. Custom does not permit privacy between them. When a young man and young woman become friends, it is assumed that marriage will eventually occur between them. It is unlikely that friendship would exist between the sexes in any other context.

Premarital contact is not condoned, though modernity is making its inroads. If the girl is found to be pregnant, the boy, and especially the boy's family, may decide that she is not worthy of marrying the son. She may either abort the baby, or she might give birth but leave the baby at the hospital for adoption. It would be uncommon for the girl to keep the baby and raise the child as a single mother. Similarly, the grandparents would not assume this responsibility either.

Once the couple decides to marry, the boy may ask the girl when he can steal or kidnap her and they will mutually decide on the date. There are many aspects to preparing for the marriage, so the girl usually has the option to establish the date for the kidnapping, though it is most common that it would be very soon. There is no period of engagement, and the wedding ceremony usually happens within weeks of the kidnapping.

The stealing event is the most significant occasion because it informs the families that they will be married. The girl must have a married female, usually a cousin or sister-in-law, as her helper to accompany her on the

---

37   King, *Ghost of Freedom*, 61.
38   Griffin, *Caucasus*, 195.

stealing. For example, the boy might call on the appointed date and ask the bride to meet him at a restaurant. The helper must accompany or meet the girl at the restaurant, and the boy may bring brothers, cousins, or friends with him. The helper is then responsible to let the girl's family members know that she has been stolen. The bride may also call her mother. Once the bride's family has been notified and the bride given the chance to agree to be kidnapped or stolen, the boy takes the girl to his family home, and the marriage is consummated that day.

The following day, the young woman can get her wedding dress, if she has not already purchased one, and other arrangements begin in earnest. The first day of the celebration must be Friday or Saturday. Friends and relatives of the boy's family are invited to his home to begin the celebration period. They will commemorate the wedding with traditional Balkarian foods for several hours. Then this entourage of the boy's family will go to the girl's family home, where they are joined by her extended family and friends. There they will spend another two to three hours. Then the entire group, except the parents, proceeds to an appointment at the local government registration office. At this ceremony the government official will validate the marriage and stamp the passports indicating the marriage relationship, and the couple may exchange rings. The government official, who may be any nationality (Russian, Kabardinian, or Balkarian), will confirm the wishes of the couple to be married, authorize the exchange of rings, and pronounce the marriage legal. The wedding party will then proceed back to the girl's family home for more food and drink.

Relatives usually give money as gifts; friends can give either money or gifts. The following day, there is continued festivity at the boy's family home, where the girl's relatives and friends continue getting to know his family. The following weekend, the merriment continues with smaller groups of relatives visiting the opposite relatives' homes to make closer acquaintance. Neither the couple nor friends participate in these visits between the families.

Interestingly, this entire process follows closely the ancient Jewish marriage ritual, where the bride and groom were paired, often by their parents, at an early age. As the bride came into the age of marriage, she would prepare for the eventuality of marriage by packing her clothing and always being ready for the coming of the groom. While she didn't know exactly when he would come, she was always ready. Once he came for her, the groom took her to his family home, to introduce her to his parents and his relatives. The actual marriage celebration took several weeks and involved the entire community of distant relatives and friends. Ultimately the bride remained in the groom's family home and became a part of his family.

For Christians the Balkarian marriage process takes on even greater significance. The Bible portrays Jesus Christ as the groom, who will come for His bride, and they will live forever in His Father's home. The bride is the entire body of believers who love and follow Jesus. At the end of time, of which no one knows the exact date or moment, the bride will be snatched away from earth. Since no sin can enter heaven, the bride must be clothed in garments of righteousness, which is the gift of Christ given to individuals when they become believers. Thus the snatching away of the bride, the introduction to the groom's family, the pristine and glorious clothing, and lengthy celebration have interesting parallels in both the Christian culture and in the Balkar culture.

While the sources for this information agree on the Balkar process as described, emotions change considerably when the situation becomes personal. I first learned of Toma's marriage from her father, Alim Kulbaev, about three months after the wedding. He had experienced deep shame, depression, and anger over his daughter's kidnapping and marriage.[39] The shame was both cultural and spiritual, as he is a Christian pastor and a Balkarian man who is very well known in the community. His daughter married a Muslim, but in addition to that shame, its timing violated another cultural tradition.

Photo 15: Toma Kulbaeva, a third-generation Balkarian, visiting America.

The very day that Toma was kidnapped, a distant relative of her father died. The Balkarian custom requires that at least one year pass after such a death before any type of celebration, especially a wedding, takes place. There should first be fifty-two days of "sadness" or mourning. This period of sadness is to be observed by the immediate and extended family. In the remainder of the North Caucasus, both the Russian Orthodox and the Muslim traditions only observe a forty-day mourning period, but the Balkarians observe fifty-two days of sadness. To ignore this custom is to bring shame on the family. It is the duty of the person whose family is involved to postpone the wedding.

Toma spoke to me about the wedding process when she visited America. Three months later she was back in her home and was stolen. She had one semester left before she would graduate from the

---

39   Alim Kulbaev, interview by author several times during March 2011, Nalchik, Kabardino-Balkaria, tape recording and transcript.

university, and was looking forward to finding a job as a teacher. She described her experience a few months after her marriage to Boris Chabdorov:

> When I arrived at the café, Boris' sisters, brothers, and friends were with him. Later, as we were all in the car driving, his sisters informed me that Boris wanted to kidnap me—today! We all drove to my home, and they told my mother and visiting aunt that they had kidnapped her daughter, and they asked me if I would agree to go with them. I had no idea of this, nor did my family. From his side, I understood that he was serious, but I didn't tell anyone in my family. Before I was kidnapped, I was thinking about this and I knew that I loved him. He had told me that he loved me, but I never told him, because I thought it might be just my feeling and he might not feel the same.

> I said yes, I would be kidnapped. If I said no, it would bring shame on him and his family, so I said yes. I knew that I wanted to marry him. I wasn't coerced. I know that he loves me and I had, and have, this same feeling for him. I didn't want to say no, because if I said no at this time, I would not have another chance. It would be too much shame for him to come to me a second time. Before I said yes, he told me I could finish the university. That was very important to me.

> The relative who died was not close to me. When he died, I asked my family who he was. I did not even know him; I had never seen him nor met him. I didn't even know of him. I didn't know he was so close to my family. When my mom and aunt came to my husband's house, they told us about the death. Boris and his family said it was okay; we could wait to have the wedding. So we waited three and a half weeks for the wedding ceremony.[40]

Toma and Boris' marriage was consummated on January 4, 2011, the date of the kidnapping. The wedding ceremony is the official government registration of the marriage, which was on January 29, 2011. The ceremony was conducted in Boris' family home, where each agreed to marry the other and rings were exchanged. A Muslim imam, who had no qualms marrying a Christian and a Muslim, presided over the ceremony. "Since I am Balkarian, they assumed I'm Muslim, so no one questioned this. Both families' relatives were at the ceremony, including my parents." Toma wore a traditional wedding dress at the first ceremony, and for the second ceremony, a week later at her parents' home, she wore a white dress but not the wedding dress. Her sister-in-law, Tamara, was her helper. Toma continued:

> My parents were very angry, as I knew they would be. My mother doesn't want to live in her house without me here. I like his family very much. His father

---

40   Toma Kulbaeva, interview by author, March 20, 2011, Nalchik, Kabardino-Balkaria, tape recording.

and brother are very good to me. I am very comfortable in their home. They told me I could sit with them, I could eat with them, and that this is now my home. I can talk with them very easily.[41]

This is in contrast to the situation in Toma's home, where her newlywed sister-in-law, Tamara, does not sit with the family, does not eat with the family, and basically lives like hired help within the household. It is the custom for the new daughter-in-law to be silent in the presence of the elders, and especially the parents-in-law. It is her duty to cook, clean, and assist in the care of her new home. Toma explained that this custom of the new bride working her way into the family is traditional and how it plays out in individual homes may be different. Her mother knew of her son's interest in Tamara, and also knew Tamara's family. However, Toma's father had no prior knowledge of the girl's family nor of his son's interest.

Toma's father was bitter and sad over his daughter's marriage. He lamented:

I'm sad not only for my shame and for the shame she has brought our family, but for the consequences of her decision. My own sisters would not even come to the wedding party because it was our time of sorrow. This decision will be known to my grandchildren, and they will not respect their father and mother for the shame caused. My son did a wrong thing [marrying outside his faith], but it was not unexpected. But I told my daughter at that time that I feared she would make a worse decision. And in only one week [after my son's marriage], she had done a worse thing.[42]

When asked how she thought her father would react once grandchildren started coming, Toma smiled shyly and whispered, "I am already pregnant!"

While bride stealing is the customary process of courtship and marriage in a culture steeped in traditions, some modern methods of dating and marrying are seeping into the Balkar mindset. Preplanning and getting to know the two families so there is acceptance of the couple is gaining ground among some of the younger Balkarians.

In fact, one unmarried young man, Ruslan Voronov, vowed he will be more considerate of the families involved by preplanning with the girl so there is acceptance, rather than stealing the girl without her foreknowledge and then surprising everyone. Ruslan faces another challenge when it comes to marriage, as his family is culturally mixed. His father is Russian and his mother is Balkarian. Ruslan notes that, as they become older, they each become more committed to their own traditions, which sometimes

---

41   Ibid.
42   Kulbaev, interview.

creates friction. Furthermore, Ruslan has become a Christian, which creates additional tension in the family that includes a Muslim mother and an atheist father. Ruslan desires to marry a Christian Balkar girl, which will bring new challenges to his family.[43]

Photo 16: Ruslan Voronov, a third-generation Balkarian.

As discussed earlier, the youngest, or only, son in the family is expected to continue to live at home, even after marriage. It is his responsibility to take care of his parents in their old age, and he then inherits the family home. Clearly, the wife of this son must assume a major responsibility in this regard, so peace in the family is very important. In Ruslan's situation, he is the only son, and as such will continue to live in the family home and care for his parents, along with the woman he brings into the family as his wife.

Madina agreed that when a couple has known each other and like each other, it is becoming more common that the boy will ask the girl, "Do you want to marry me?" If she agrees to marry, he then steals her. "I think the bride's parents accept bride stealing as their tradition, and they realize it will probably happen." However, Madina estimates that

> probably half of our weddings are not connected to bride stealing; the couple agrees ahead of time and plans the wedding with both parents. Most of the remainder of marriages occur at least with the agreement of the girl.[44]

Society does not necessarily encourage large families. It is not uncommon to wait until the late twenties or early thirties to marry, so Balkar families are usually small. Abortions are accepted in Balkarian society if a woman is married and doesn't want any more children. It is not considered a shame unless the woman is unmarried.

Divorces are relatively easy in Balkarian society. Traditionally the husband initiated the divorce, though now women can also begin divorce proceedings. If there are no children under eighteen years, the couple may apply to the government registration office and the divorce is granted. If there are children under eighteen, or if there are disputes regarding property, a divorce request will be sent to the court. There is a six-month waiting

43   Ruslan Voronov, interview by author, March 19, 2011, Yanikoi, Kabardino-Balkaria, tape recording and transcript.
44   Zhanataeva, interview.

period, which allows time for a resolution. Mothers are awarded custody of children unless there are criminal, drug, or alcohol issues. The father is required to pay child support until children reach eighteen years, or twenty-three if they attend the university, and the father always has visitation rights.

Both weddings and funerals are events which are steeped in traditions and which test a fledgling Christian church in a Muslim nation. As a Balkarian Christian pastor, Alim Kulbaev said:

> There are so few Christians in this nation that we have limited experience in creating separate, Christian traditions. The national traditions, many of which are Muslim, are very hard to challenge. Furthermore, we have had only a few weddings or deaths among the Christians.[45]

Additionally, funerals and burials are the responsibility of the family. If the family is Muslim and the deceased is a Christian, the family's desires will take precedence over the faith of the deceased. Alim continued:

> The church does not have enough power or influence to dictate the funeral proceedings, so we abide by the elders of the clan for the deceased person. We are simply too "young" as a group of believers. Even when a Christian dies, the elders of the clan have more power than the Muslim imam and can mandate burial of the non-Muslim in the Muslim cemetery.[46]

Photo 17: Tombstones in a Russian cemetery.

"Tremendous importance is placed upon a man being buried in his village, next to all his ancestors."[47] While a person can sign a last will and testament indicating his funeral preferences, the family will ultimately decide. That is why, when relatives desire a Muslim burial, Alim continued, "We don't push back, because we believe the body will deteriorate but the spirit will be raised in Christ. We always honor the family's preference."[48]

Thus the Balkar funeral rituals generally follow Islamic customs. If a person dies after noon, he must be buried before noon the next day. If he dies before noon, he must be buried by sunset the same day. The body is shaved and washed by family members of the same sex. The body is wrapped in two pieces of cloth like a blanket, then placed on a gurney and taken outside the home. The local Islamic clergy comes to the home and delivers

45   Kulbaev, interview.
46   Ibid.
47   Griffin, *Caucasus*, 22.
48   Kulbaev, interview.

a sermon, reminding those present that all will return to their Creator, and those present are asked to forgive any debts owed by the deceased. The men then go to the cemetery to bury the deceased. Women are excluded, even if the deceased is a woman, because of the custom of separation of men and women, and also because "women are too emotional. Men have a duty to bury the body, and the women can go to the cemetery later," Alim concluded.[49] Friends and relatives gather at the home and share good and happy stories about the deceased. And the fifty-two days of sorrow begins.

Photo 18: Tombstones in a Balkarian village cemetery.

Many of the cemeteries portray visible reminders of the deceased. The headstones indicate the birth and death dates, and often include an engraved photo of the deceased. This practice occurs in both Russian and Balkar cemeteries.

---

49   Ibid.

4
Political/Societal Structures

Historically, there were different political structures among the many ethnic societies of the North Caucasus. Some, such as the Balkars' neighbors, the Kabardinians, were organized according to an intricate feudal hierarchy. Others were organized with religious (Muslim) rulers. Still others were ruled by hereditary lineage. The upland villages of the Balkars were often led by a village elder or council, with social power more dispersed.

To understand the various peoples, it is important to evaluate the degree to which political and economic power is concentrated in the hands of a few or dispersed within the group, rather than using typical organizational or political labels. The most difficult aspect of understanding the North Caucasus peoples is the fact that no one person, nor one group, had authority over or represented all of these mountain peoples. Each ethnic group related to Russia individually since, over the years, Russia battled against specific, individual Caucasus nations. Some parts of the Caucasus were easily integrated into the Russian Empire, while others, particularly in the highlands, were more resistant to submitting to Russian control.

Traditions are rooted deep within the Balkarian culture, with everyone understanding how things should be. There are expectations of behavior, which are an extension of the Islamic honor/shame-based philosophy. The Islamic and traditional values converge to create intense resistance to outside influence of any sort, whether social, political, economic, or spiritual. The *tawhid*, the Islamic doctrine that confirms the oneness of Allah, is also reflected in all aspects of Balkarian society and culture. The Balkar village culture operates as a "oneness," an enforced uniformity or conformity. This is a highly revered and protected value. Additionally, the Balkars are historically xenophobic, reflecting the highest level of closedness, distrust, suspicion, and resistance to the outside world, to other cultures, and to other ways of thinking. These two characteristics—conformity and xenophobia—combine to keep any hints of modernization, any intrusion of contrary views, especially spiritual or secular values, from entering the cocoon of their beliefs. Recent developments in Russia reveal

> an undisguised racist contempt and suspicion toward ethnic minorities, espe-cially Caucasians . . . Discrimination in the workplace and harassment from police . . . has contributed to trends among the non-Russian minorities: to remain as much as possible within their own ethnic territory; to try to increase

ethnic power and autonomy within those territories; to consolidate their economic and social position at the expense of the local Russian population; and to resuscitate their traditional culture, native language, and, in this case, their Islamic faith.[50]

The revered ancestral customs and laws, the *adats*, were passed down orally for centuries. The *adats* centered on the abilities of clans and families to deal with their own. The Balkars' tradition of natural democracy, of allowing anyone to speak on matters of interest to the community, has survived over the centuries. Ultimately the elders continue to be more influential in their communities than the government. They solve the problems of the community without the help of the police, and they help the poor among them without the assistance of the government.

The Islamic law of vendetta requires retaliation. "Revenge is a right and an honour. It was not so much as an eye for eye and tooth for tooth as eyes for eye and teeth for tooth." This law evokes fear more than it practices revenge; that fear will temper responses so that no highlander will casually insult another. However, "the problem with the vendetta is that once started, it is hard to stop. There are many examples within Caucasian history of blood feuds going back four and five generations."[51]

50   S. A. Arutiunov, "Ethnicity in the Caucasus: Ethnic Relations and Quasi-ethnic Conflicts," Circassian World, accessed August 20, 2010, http://www.circassianworld.com/new/north-caucasus/1175-ethnic-conflicts-caucasus.html.

51   Griffin, *Caucasus*, 23.

5
Spirituality

While all of the peoples within the North Caucasus region, except the Ossetians, are labeled Muslims, their adherence to Islam varies significantly. Islam was first introduced into the eastern portion of the Caucasus in the mid-eighth century. Due to the trade routes and periods of conquest by the Ottomans and the Persians, Islam was spread throughout the Caucasus nations with varying degrees of success. Islam was more deeply entrenched among the peoples of the eastern Caucasus; as one travels west, the role of Islam was less evident, and to the northwest, Islam was only nominally accepted by the various peoples.

> Throughout their history, the North Caucasus remained on the fringes of the Islamic world. The neighboring Ottoman and Persian Empires had never succeeded in conquering and annexing the region and remained content with collecting payments in tribute, taxes, and slaves rather than assimilating the peoples into their cultures.[52]

The peoples of the North Caucasus represent a highly fragmented aggregation of societies organized on the basis of kinship, language, and common territory, with their primary reliance on the *adats*. The Balkarians were pagan animists from their earliest history. There is Jewish influence dating back to 586 BC, when the Persians deported the Jews of Israel and scattered them throughout the known world at that time. There is strong evidence of Christianity among the Balkars given their mythology and toponymy, the scientific study of Balkar place names. The names of the months of the year and days of the week also demonstrate an early Christian influence. However, by the late 1300s, invasions by Tamerlan effectively destroyed the Christian church in much of Asia.

Islam did not become the definitive religion among the Balkars until the beginning of the nineteenth century. When Islam was introduced, it was confronted by these traditional religious practices in addition to other religions. In analyzing traditions from the past,

> religious differences had only a relatively superficial effect on the local folk literature, since most of the ethnic groups in the mountains had passed through a series of religious changes, resulting in mixtures of pagan, Moslem and

---

52   Michael Khodarkovsky, "The Indigenous Elites and the Construction of Ethnic Identities in the North Caucasus," Circassian World, accessed July 17, 2011, http://www.circassianworld.com/new/north-caucasus/1169-indigenous-elites-khodarkovsky.html.

Christian traditions . . . By studying the mythological ideas and beliefs of the Caucasus peoples one cannot avoid the thought that there used to exist in the Caucasus one religion, which was subsequently obscured.[53]

Traces of these pagan concepts can still be seen in rituals of the Balkars today, with Islamic eschatology with its terminology and customs only recently becoming a part of the Balkar religious fabric.

"Festivals were, as in most animist religions, based on the seasons of the natural world: moon, harvests, snows. Grapes and milk were fermented, then drunk."[54] It was not until the late 1800s that the Muslim prohibition of alcohol was introduced. However, the ban on alcohol is not widely adhered to, as both alcohol and drug abuse are major problems in the Balkar society.

Traditions that are considered Balkarian supersede any named religion. Several of the local people emphasized that they are Muslim only in name, only in tradition. In fact, unlike other areas of the world where the Islamic faith has assumed predominance in every aspect of life, the Balkarians have practiced it more as a folk religion, integrating aspects of the Muslim faith into their traditions. The veneration of local saints, sacred trees, springs, and other forms of nature combined with Islam to create a form of folk Islam unique to the region.

An example of the syncretization of faiths is seen as one travels the highlands today. Thousands of strips of cloth, resembling a myriad of bandages, tied on the branches of trees surrounding a makeshift mosque will be noticed on the landscape. "They are prayer rags, marks of intent, and are found not just outside mosques but also around Christian churches in the Caucasus. Beliefs are strong in the mountains—they run deeper and longer than organized religion; rituals still repeated, if not understood."[55]

These prayer rags are reminiscent of the practice at the western wall of the Jewish temple in Jerusalem, where the cracks are filled with tiny pieces of paper bearing the requests of the people. Christianity and Judaism among some upland tribal groups were able to modify Islam with traditional practices to suit their own local traditions. Thus the notion that the entire Balkarian nationality has been historically Muslim is somewhat of a misnomer.

Under communism, religion was outlawed. Religious activities went underground or were discarded. It is of interest, however, that during the brief Nazi occupation of Nalchik, the KBR capital, the traditional Muslim holiday marking the end of Ramadan occurred. To appease the people, the

---

53   David Hunt, "Colour Symbolism in the Folk Literature of the Caucasus," *Folklore* 117 (December 2006): 330.

54   Griffin, *Caucasus*, 22.

55   Ibid., 74.

Nazis allowed its commemoration in 1942. People from the villages sent "gifts of poultry, wine, fruit, sweets, national costumes, and a select group of the most attractive male and female dancers. At a later time, this celebration [of Kurman] served as one of the bases for the charge of treason against the Balkars."[56] If indeed the religious practices of the Muslims had been totally discarded under communism, there would not have been such an open celebration of Kurman during the Great Patriotic War.

Nekrich points out that the surface friendliness of the Balkars toward the Nazis was only due to their short stay in the region.

> It was not because the Nazis had succeeded in winning over the Caucasian people . . . [In other occupied regions] looting, physical maltreatment, and discrimination were widespread. Economic exploitation was attempted on a wide scale. In cases of doubt, military demands had priority over indigenous interests. German reprisals for killings or pillage of army stocks were as swift and savage as elsewhere in occupied Europe.[57]

---

56   Aleksandr M. Nekrich, *The Punished Peoples: The Deportation and Fate of Soviet Minorities at the End of the Second World War* (New York: Norton, 1978), 62.

57   Ibid., 85.

6
The Cult of Stalin

Joseph Stalin was able to do what no other leader in Russia's history had been able to accomplish. Under his leadership the entire North Caucasus region became officially part of the Russian Empire, becoming known as the Union of Soviet Socialist Republics (USSR). Was his destructive drive for power due to some deep character traits whose roots were themselves deeply imbedded in his own South Caucasus origins? Perhaps his intimate knowledge of the Caucasus peoples sparked him to pursue policies which would bind them to the USSR. King argues that such comparisons fail, as there were many other Georgians, and people from the Caucasus in general, who did not follow such a path of violence and destruction to accomplish their goals.

> The mere existence of alternatives to Bolshevism points to the fact that there is little in the Caucasus itself to explain Stalin's political pathologies or the callousness with which he dealt with his homeland once he had consolidated his power in Moscow.[58]

In fact, he spent most of his life and career outside of the Caucasus region and committed a grave, culturally unforgivable, shameful act when he failed to return to his homeland for his mother's funeral.

Stalin was raised in Georgia, in the southern Caucasus Mountains, by a domineering Georgian mother who was an Ossetian Christian. His father was absent from his life for the most part. Stalin's formative adolescence was infused by the macho clannishness of Georgian society. He studied for the priesthood and wrote poetry. He was obsessed with loyalty, betrayal, and secrecy. Stalin was a solitary man and allowed very few people, including family members, to become close to him. He was captivated with the intrigue of treason, betrayal, and methods of using those charges to punish those he felt opposed him. As one who preferred to operate in the shadows, Stalin utilized over twenty aliases over his lifetime. "He put it best himself: 'Before the Revolution [of 1917 against the tsars], our Party led an underground existence—a secret Party. Now circumstances have changed'—and they did not really suit him. He flourished in the shadows."[59] Others noted that he was

---

58 King, *Ghost of Freedom*, 183.
59 Simon Sebag Montefiore, *Young Stalin* (London: Weidenfeld & Nicolson, 2007), 332.

very valuable behind the scenes . . . He did have the knack of convincing the average run of leaders . . . He wasn't regarded as the official leader of the Party . . . but everyone listened to what he had to say, including Lenin—he was a representative of the rank and file, one who expressed its real views and moods . . . [and he was] the unquestioned leader of the Caucasians.[60]

He ultimately did not view himself as a son of the Caucasus, but rather as a quadrinational: Georgian by nationality, Russian by loyalty, international by ideology, Soviet by citizenship. In fact, Caucasians would not claim him as their own due to his violation of the Caucasus ethnic values: disloyalty to his friends and family, dishonor to his native people, and lack of commitment to his homeland.

By the time of the First Central Committee of the Communist Party meeting in 1911, "Lenin now recognized that Stalin was one of the few Bolsheviks who shared his keenness to formulate policies that would win followers amongst the non-Russian peoples of the empire, but without promising them independence."[61] Lenin wanted to offer autonomy and the right to secession to these nationalities, but he had no intention of actually granting these rights.

Stalin satisfied this need through his most famous work, *Marxism and the National Question,* published in 1913, which outlined his philosophy toward the nationalities throughout the Russian Empire. In this article, using one of his many aliases, Stalin gave his definition of the difference between nations and tribes, races, linguistic groups, or people who simply occupied the same land. He defined a nation as historically evolved and stable, which could include its own language, territory, economic life, and psychological makeup. He also believed that the definition of a nation could evolve over time; nothing was forever. And while he asserted that the policy of self-determination was appropriate to all nations, he specifically denied that right to the peoples of the Caucasus, calling it "meaningless and nonsensical in relation to Caucasian conditions." He denied that the nations of the Caucasus were real nations, calling them "'peoples,' some with literary languages and others with only primitive dialects; some with a coherent economic system and others with only barter and the bazaar."[62] And further, any test of genuine nationhood must be analyzed under the rubric of what was best for the workers rather than the wealthy class. He felt that any practices that were hostile "to the improvement of the workers' lot—such as the veiling of women in Muslim lands—would have to be eliminated in a socialist state."[63]

---

60   Ibid., 334.
61   Ibid., 250.
62   King, *Ghost of Freedom,* 185.
63   Ibid., 186.

Stalin created a web of seven republics in the North Caucasus region, offering these nations the illusion of autonomy, calling them "autonomous republics"with the right to secede. This "remains relevant because the breakup of the Soviet Union in 1991 allowed the full republics such as Ukraine, Estonia and Georgia to become independent but not the autonomous republics," including the Kabardino-Balkaria Autonomous Republic.[64]

In October 1917 Lenin persuaded Stalin to become the People's Commissar of Nationalities, a role he served until 1923. Lenin, Stalin's hero, regarded Stalin as an aggressor,

> a vulgar Great Russian bully ... Lenin was concerned about preserving the multinational state and the influence its example could have in the future on the nations of Asia ... [He] understood clearly that crudity or injustice ... toward our own (non-Russian nationalities) would reflect negatively on the authority of the Soviet state among the peoples of Asia.[65]

According to Aleksandr Nekrich, "Lenin's idea of 'cultural assistance' to the smaller nations by the former oppressor nation, so that each small nation can construct its 'own state' was absolutely correct."[66] However, these ideas collided with the realities of the centralization philosophy of communism, as it sought to strengthen the power of the state.

> Energetic social reorganization without any special allowance for the particular national features and conditions of each people ... [intensified] all the contradictions in the life of the state as a whole and without exception. Under such conditions the rise of conflicts between small and large nations became inevitable, up to and including armed clashes [which included Georgia, Chechnya, South Ossetia, and ongoing skirmishes to the present day].[67]

In summary, the collision of Lenin's idealistic support of small nationalities with the centralization philosophy of communism found its culmination within the cult of Stalin, with the centralization practice prevailing.

---

64   Montefiore, *Young Stalin*, 277.
65   Nekrich, *Punished Peoples*, 100–101.
66   Ibid., 177.
67   Ibid.

7
Evolution of Nations or Affirmative Action?

The long-term goal of the Soviet regime was based on the Marxist theory of changing the economic base in order to accomplish social reform, bringing all of the citizenry of the Soviet Union under communism. However, all of the different and diverse people groups within the borders of the Soviet Union were not at the same level of societal development. Thus the Bolsheviks determined to develop and accelerate the historical development process of the peoples simultaneously with changing the economic methodology of society.

Beginning in the 1920s the effort was focused on taking feudal-era clans and tribes to a consciousness of their own national identity, which Francine Hirsch calls the evolution of nations. The goal of state-sponsored evolutionism was not self-determination for the nations, nor was it making nations for their own sake. Hirsch argues that this

> state-sponsored evolution was not a form of "affirmative action" intended to promote "national minorities" at the expense of "national majorities" . . . [but rather a policy] to "assist" the potential victims of *Soviet* economic modernization, and thus to differentiate the Soviet state from the "imperialistic empires" [of Europe] it disdained.[68]

In order to accomplish this, the Soviets forged alliances and secured loyalties of the local elites and leaders in the North Caucasus region and

> introduced administrative and social structures that encouraged or demanded mass participation. No issue was more central to the formation of the Soviet Union than the nationality question . . . The Bolsheviks had called for the national self-determination of all peoples and had condemned all forms of colonization as exploitative.[69]

These local leaders were trained to become party workers at the local level and were instrumental in advancing the communist agenda of the Bolsheviks in their local territories. By relying on local leaders that were installed in positions of the government, the party, industry, and schools, the Bolsheviks were able to attribute their actions as the will of the people.

---

68   Hirsch, *Empire of Nations*, 8.
69   Ibid., 5.

The Soviet effort to change society was advanced by accelerating the evolution of the population through the stages of historical development along Marxist lines. Hirsch agrees with other scholars that

the Bolsheviks took state-sponsored evolutionism very seriously, putting far more effort into realizing its ends than the European colonial empires had put into their own civilizing missions. Characterizing "backwardness" a result of sociohistorical circumstances and not of innate racial or biological traits, Soviet leaders maintained that all peoples could "evolve" and thrive in the new Soviet conditions.[70]

Terry Martin argues that this policy of developing nations was actually affirmative action, rather than the evolution of nations. The Soviet regime supported *preferential* treatment of the nationalities throughout all of the USSR, not *equal* treatment as is implied by Hirsch. In fact, the policies clearly downplayed and stigmatized "Russian national culture and identity while promoting non-Russian identity."[71] The Soviet refusal to create its own nationality, incorporating all of the indigenous nations into a new nation was a major principle of its affirmative action policy. They believed that

all ethnic groups, no matter how small, should not be forced to assimilate . . . and should be granted national forms . . . Russian culture and Russian national interest were de-emphasized so as not to threaten the mistrustful non-Russians and provoke defensive nationalism.[72]

Thus the affirmative action program was not only to prepare these peoples for incorporation into a communist society, but also to make the nationalities look attractive to their ethnic brethren across the borders.

While disagreeing on the terminology, both scholars do agree that the Soviet treatment of the people groups demonstrated a commitment to territories inhabited by specific nationalities, developing and using their own languages as a priority over the Russian language, identification and promotion of their own national cultures, and with their own elites providing the leadership in their territories (under the central government control).

The Soviet nationalities policy demanded that all education and government work be conducted in native languages. Since the written languages of the majority of the Soviet Union's small nationalities were in a very rudimentary state, this created a sudden need for rapid linguistic reform.[73]

---

70   Ibid., 9.
71   Terry Martin, *The Affirmative Action Empire: Nations and Nationalism in the Soviet Union, 1923–1939* (New York: Cornell University Press, 2001), 178.
72   Ibid., 203.
73   Ibid., 185.

The Soviets also promoted museums that displayed the cultural accomplishments of the nationalities as well as highlighting their cultural traditions. The creation of borders for each nationality contributed to the developing self-awareness and self-identity of the individual nationalities.

Initially the Soviets focused on the building of the nations throughout the USSR, coining the term *natsionalizatsiia*. Stalin used this phrase throughout his life because it emphasized nation building. However, by 1923 the term *korenitzatsiia* became the official government term for the combination of all of these policies of nation building, and was "part of the Bolsheviks' decolonizing rhetoric, which systematically favored the claims of indigenous peoples."[74]

The development of affirmative action in the North Caucasus region was carried out by the local leadership and ratified by the central government. This author agrees with the arguments of Martin that these policies were indeed affirmative action on the part of the Soviets in their efforts to achieve their goals of attracting people to communism within its borders, and in the countries across its borders, as well as communicating a broader decolonizing message to the world. The Soviets had established a course of action through its affirmative action policies to prove that communism was the best method of organizing and governing nations.

---

74   Ibid., 12.

8
The Piedmont Principle
Collides with Soviet Xenophobia

In 1923 the affirmative action policy, called *korenitzatsiia* (nation building), toward national minorities in the border regions was reaffirmed and emphasized. The implementation mandated more national schools, more national territories, an expanded native-language press, aggressive recruitment and promotion of national cadres, and strict punishment of all Russian chauvinism. The Soviet government consciously aimed to emphasize and promote the ethnic diversity of the border regions. "It was the Soviet leadership's strong commitment to forming a multinational state, rather than any hostility to ethnic identities, that politicized ethnicity by linking it to the formation of administrative territories, land possession, and resettlement."[75]

This policy of nation building was based on the Piedmont Principle, a term coined by Terry Martin, which was the conspicuous benevolence toward the border nationalities within the Soviet Union. It took affirmative action one step further in its effort to present and promote the superiority of the Soviet way of life to the neighboring countries across its borders. Special privileges, increased salaries, more economic investment, a better supply of goods, and cultural investment were among the tactics employed by the Soviets to promote their foreign policy goals of exploiting cross-border ethnic ties to project Soviet influence abroad. Martin examined the contradictions inherent in the Soviet nationality policy, which sought simultaneously to foster the growth of national consciousness among its minority populations while eliminating all foreign influence on the Soviet Union's many nationalities, both within the Soviet Union and around the world.

> [During this] early Soviet period, even voluntary assimilation was actively discouraged. The Soviet regime devoted considerable resources to the promotion of the national self-consciousness of its non-Russian populations. Each Soviet nation, no matter how small, was granted its own national territory, national schools, and national elites.[76]

The Soviets created and encouraged use of their native languages.

---

75   Martin, "Origins," 829.
76   Ibid., 816.

This commitment to ethnic proliferation would seem to have made the Soviet Union a highly unlikely site for the emergence of ethnic cleansing . . . [which ultimately devolved] to a repressive policy featuring ethnic deportations, national terror and russification.[77]

Scholars agree that the attempt to develop and define ethnic identities took place in the early Soviet times. Michael Khordarkovsky attributes the failure of the nation-building program to the Soviet antireligious policies.

The most potent force which worked against the emergence of the ethnic identities in the North Caucasus [in the early twentieth century] was a [sic] religion of Islam, which attempted to unify the peoples of the region on the basis of an Islamic identity against its main antagonist, the Russian empire.[78]

However, the tension between the nationalities, as well as the disparate adherence to, and identification with, Islam among the nationalities contributed to the failure of the nation-building efforts as well.

Ultimately the Piedmont Policy produced an unintended tension between the border nations and the Soviet government, as the inherent paranoia of Stalin and his colleagues took priority. Soviet xenophobia was manifested in the "exaggerated Soviet fear of foreign influence and foreign contamination . . . [It] was ideological, not ethnic. It was spurred by the ideological hatred and suspicion of foreign capitalist governments, not the national hatred of non-Russians."[79] Ongoing uprisings and low-intensity guerrilla warfare occurred along the Soviet frontier, which deepened the fears of foreign penetration and focused Soviet xenophobia on its border regions which were inhabited by other ethnicities, including the North Caucasus border.

In 1923 the Soviet government delineated a special, continuous administrative territory, called the border regions, and established a series of increasingly high-security border strips running along the entire land and sea border of the Soviet Union. This decree focused exclusively on defensive security measures to keep out foreign influence. Thus the Soviet xenophobia, on the one hand encouraging ethnic suspicions across the borders, conflicted with the Piedmont Principle, which was to promote Soviet life across the borders. The Piedmont Principle worked at cross purposes with the Soviet xenophobia.

Two specific assaults on the policies of the Soviet government prepared the way for the ethnic cleansing that was to come. First was the collective farming policies, and second was the response to these policies by the masses of people trying to emigrate from the USSR. The Soviet program of collectivization started in 1928–29. As private farm land was confiscated by

---

77   Ibid.
78   Khodarkovsky, "Indigenous Elites."
79   Martin, *Affirmative Action Empire*, 313.

the Soviet government, the *sharia* (Muslim) law was abolished, the population was disarmed, and the Caucasian political and intellectual leadership was annihilated or deported, accused of trying to turn the people against the Soviet government. The grain production quotas alone drove many to leave the Central Asia and Caucasus regions of the USSR to seek better conditions in other countries.

The most significant emigration attempt was in 1929 when 4,500 Russian Germans requested exit visas to leave the Soviet Union. The Soviets denied their applications, and the Germans appealed to the German consulate. At that point the international news media publicized their situation. The repressive policies of the Soviet government became international news, and the situation was a huge embarrassment to the Soviets. Ethnic uprisings spread throughout the nations and inspired additional emigration movements from 1929 to 1930. These movements vividly challenged the Soviet leadership with the failure of the Piedmont Principle. The national minorities were meant to be attractive communist examples to their ethnic brethren abroad; instead they turned toward their home countries, repudiating the Soviets in an exceedingly embarrassing fashion. Additionally, these ethnic minorities were not easily coerced into the collectivization program, creating additional resistance to the Soviet policies. Several uprisings in border regions continued to concern the Soviet government about the loyalty and security of these lands. The Soviet response was to put additional resources and pressure to increase the implementation of the collectivization program.

Tensions continued to mount until 1933, when the Ukrainian terror resulted in the arrests of thousands of Ukrainian nationals. The grain harvest was insufficient for the USSR, leading it into the Great Famine of 1932–33. Stalin blamed the farmers for stealing the grain. The government's response was to seize even more than the required amount from the grain-growing regions of the North Caucasus (and Ukraine) in order to address the shortage of food. The government's priority was to feed the urban dwellers at the expense of the farmers in the rural areas. The Piedmont Principle was thus abandoned, and Stalin adopted a policy of excluding all foreign influence, making the Soviet Union a fortress against such infiltration.

The famine from the food shortages not only ended the Piedmont policies; it also introduced the practice of mass deportation based on ethnicity. The first ethnic deportation was an entire town of Ukrainian nationals; they had allegedly sabotaged a grain delivery. Ultimately, two more towns of Ukrainians and a total of over sixty thousand people were displaced from their homeland based on their ethnicity. They were replaced by "14,090 Red Army soldiers and their families."[80] These deportations marked the beginning of ethnic-based deportations, which dominated Soviet policy from 1933 to 1953, as opposed to class-based deportations, which was the norm prior to 1933.

The famine also ushered in the Great Terror, a period from 1935 to 1938 when "approximately 800,000 individuals were arrested, deported, or executed in the ethnic cleansing and mass national operations."[81] The roots of Soviet ethnic cleansing are an important part of the origin of the Great Terror as by 1938 the Great Terror had evolved into an ethnic terror.

Martin concluded that the "Soviet turn toward ethnic cleansing in the 1930s was not even accompanied by a trend favoring assimilation, but rather by an increased emphasis on the distinct primordial essence of the Soviet Union's nationalities."[82] Even voluntary assimilation, or integration, into the Russian culture was forbidden. Martin's theory on the Soviets' increased emphasis on the nationalities, even when it appeared to be failing, considered three points:

> First, the Soviet leadership was already committed to ethnic resettlement in the 1920s to promote ethnic consolidation and the formation of national territories . . .

> Second, popular ethnic hostility played a role in the origins of Soviet ethnic cleansing, . . . [as] some of the most important diaspora nationalities within the Soviet Union (Ukrainians, Koreans, Germans, Finns, Poles) became the targets of popular ethnic hostility. This hostility led to harsh treatment during collectivization, which helped provoke the mass emigration movements, . . . [and resulted in local Communists stigmatizing these groups] . . .

> Third, . . . the Soviet belief in the political salience of ethnicity, which was reflected in the government's entire policy of supporting national institutions, led to its adoption of the Piedmont Principle: the attempt to exploit cross-border ethnic ties to project influence abroad. However, the exaggerated Soviet fear of foreign capitalist influence and contamination—. . . Soviet xenophobia—also made cross-border ties potentially suspect . . . [He concludes that it was] Soviet, not Russian, xenophobia that drove the practice of Soviet ethnic cleansing.[83]

---

80   Martin, "Origins," 846.
81   Ibid., 858.
82   Ibid., 859.
83   Ibid., 859–61.

9
Ethnic Cleansing or Genocide?

There is some debate as to whether the deportation of entire nationalities constituted genocide or ethnic cleansing. "Ethnic cleansing" refers to the forcible removal of an ethnically defined population from a given territory, usually for the purpose of removing a stigmatized ethnic group.[84] "Genocide," on the other hand, offers a range of definitions, from the extermination of an entire population in the most extreme case, to the establishment of circumstances that will not necessarily physically eliminate a people but will abolish their distinct ethnic identity. Interestingly, the original definition of genocide in 1944 focused on the abolition of the group's identity, rather than mass murder of the entire group, by destruction of their cultural institutions and forced assimilation of the group to the majority culture. Thus the cultural health of the nationality would be permanently compromised, but the entire population would not necessarily be destroyed. Two years later the United Nations (UN) used this definition in its condemnation of genocide. However, in 1948, after much debate in the UN, the definition was narrowed to focus on the actual elimination of a nationality, rather than the eradication of their culture as a component of genocide.

J. Otto Pohl describes several definitions and examples of genocide. The key to genocide is the *intent* to exterminate a specific group either by killing all of the groups' members or by the destruction of a group's ethnic identity and viability, but not necessarily killing all members of the group. The large number of deaths among national groups deported to special settlements by the Soviets raises the question of genocide and the intent behind the deportations. Citing three cases of true genocide in the twentieth century, "Turkey's attempt to exterminate the Armenian people; Nazi Germany's attempted annihilation of Europe's Jews and Gypsies; and the Hutu majority government of Rwanda's systematic attempt to murder every member of its Tutsi minority," Pohl notes that in these cases, "the total extermination of the victim nationality was halted only by the military defeat of the perpetrating state."[85]

Pohl argues that the case for genocide of the deported nationalities is supported by several facts of the deportations. "The Soviet government sought to destroy these groups as distinct ethnic identities . . . [through] a

---

84   Ibid., 817.
85   J. Otto Pohl, *Ethnic Cleansing in the USSR, 1937–1949* (Westport, CT: Greenwood Press, 1999), 2.

mixture of lethal and non-lethal means."[86] The Stalin regime deliberately put the deported nationalities into conditions that it knew would bring about their physical destruction. Pohl contends that "there can be no doubt that the deportation constituted acts of ethnically motivated mass murder, [and that the] ultimate goal of these policies was to dissolve the national identities of the deported ethnic groups."[87] He concludes that "the deportation of whole nationalities to areas with deadly living conditions clearly meets the UN definition of genocide."[88]

In fact the Russian government has admitted that the Soviets committed genocide eleven times between 1937 and 1953. In 1991 Chairman Boris Yeltsin publicly acknowledged that the deportations and exile of the "Repressed Peoples" did constitute genocide.[89] More recently, on the anniversary of the Balkar deportation, March 8, 2010, the president of the Kabardino-Balkaria Republic, Arsen Kanokov, a Kabardinian, referred to the deportation as "genocide" of the Balkar people, a stronger term than when he described it as a "monstrous crime" one year earlier in 2009.[90]

Brian Glynn Williams contends that the Soviet deportation program did indeed have the *intent* to eliminate entire ethnic groups. He cites Operation Deportation, which allowed Stalin to take "advantage of the war time mobilization of Soviet troops and general distrust of non-Slavic minorities in many echelons of the Kremlin to eradicate several ethnies deemed to be untrustworthy by the Soviet regime."[91]

In the absence of scholarly consensus on what the term "genocide" should denote, this book uses the definition of genocide as the actual destruction of the significant portion of a group's members combined with the intent to destroy the group's national identity. Martin has identified five major traits generally present in ethnic cleansing:

---

86   J. Otto Pohl, "Stalin's Genocide against the 'Repressed Peoples,'" *Journal of Genocide Research* 2, no. 2 (2000): 271.

87   Ibid., 268.

88   Ibid., 289.

89   Ibid., 268.

90   Liz Fuller, "KBR President Condemns 'Genocide' of Balkars," Radio Free Europe / Radio Liberty, Circassian World, March 8, 2010, accessed July 16, 2011, http://www.circassianworld.com/new/headlines/1446-kanokov-condemns-genocide-of-balkars.html.

91   Brian Glynn Williams, "Hidden Ethnocide in the Soviet Muslim Borderlands," *Journal of Genocide Research* 4, no. 3 (2002): 358.

1. **Ethnic cleansing is the forcible removal with or without the intent of mass murder.**

In analyzing the ethnic cleansing by the Soviets, most experts concur that it was not done with the *intent* of mass murder, even though thousands of deaths resulted from the actual deportation as well as in the special settlements. Further, the Soviets' experience of deportation in the 1930s had demonstrated clearly that resettling people to hostile environments would result in substantial deaths. Thus the Soviets are clearly not innocent in the issue of mass murder, for this indeed is what happened. However, this author asserts that the *intent* was not mass murder, as the regime was capable of attaining that goal with executions, imprisonment, or relocation to the Soviet labor camps. The *intent* was to secure the borders, to punish those who interfered with the state's mandates, and to create fear and submission among the remaining population.

2. **Ethnic cleansing is usually carried out by trained professionals, such as military, security, or police.**

The deportations of the 1940s in the USSR were carried out with extreme efficiency, surprise, and speed by members of the military and secret police. Coordinating the transportation, housing, food supply, and jobs in the special settlements took enormous resources, particularly as it took place while the Soviet Union was at war against Germany.

3. **Ethnic cleansing may be the partial or total removal of a targeted people.**

The Soviet deportations targeted removal of entire peoples based solely on their ethnicity. Again the *intent* was not necessarily extermination of these peoples, but rather punishment and compliance of the citizens.

4. **Ethnic cleansing may expel the targeted people to their homes or nations abroad, or resettle them internally.**

The Soviet deportations resettled all of the exiled peoples internally, generally away from the borders and in areas that needed manpower in order to develop the socialist economy. The deportations were not simply an imprisonment, though there were strict controls on the deportees. There were many motivations for the locations to which they were deported; cheap labor and the development of these locations were especially crucial, particularly during wartime when so many men who would have been laborers were away fighting in World War II, or the Great Patriotic War as it was called in the Soviet Union.

5. Ethnic cleansing may occur during war or peace.
The ethnic cleansing of the Balkars took place during the Great Patriotic War, but Stalin's policies of ethnic cleansing continued until his death in 1956.[92]

> The emergence of the category of enemy nation and the practice of ethnic cleansing was one of the most momentous developments in the Soviet nationalities policy of the mid-1930s. Between 1935 and 1938, at least nine Soviet nationalities . . . were all subjected to ethnic cleansing (that is, the forcible relocation of an ethnically defined population away from a given territory) . . . [In the later 1930s many of the] nationalities were labeled enemy nations and specifically targeted for arrest and execution due solely to their ethnic identity . . . Ethnic cleansing, however, has typically been an extreme manifestation of the nationalist project of making state borders coincide with ethnic borders . . . The Soviet Union was not a nation-state, nor was its leadership ever committed to turning it into a nation-state. No attempt was made to forge a new Soviet nationality, and even voluntary assimilation was strongly discouraged. The Soviet regime devoted considerable resources to the promotion of the national self-consciousness of its non-Russian populations.[93]

The Soviet policy of the 1920s of building nations juxtaposed against the deportations of nations makes the Soviet Union an unlikely candidate for the emergence of ethnic cleansing.

> The simultaneous pursuit of nation-building and the nation-destroying in the 1930s is a paradox . . . [However, Martin argues that the] same principles that informed Soviet nation-building in the 1920s . . . [led] to the ethnic cleansing and ethnic terror against a limited set of stigmatized nationalities, while leaving nation-building policies in place for the majority of non-stigmatized nationalities.[94]

Stalin and his close group of deputies used the purge as an effective tool for ridding the state and the Communist Party of real or perceived rivals. This mechanism allowed the government to control society, to test the loyalty of party members, and to eliminate adversaries. They had discovered a template to be used in dealing with those who deviated from the policies set down by Stalin and his associates. The party was returning to its origins as a relatively small, conspiratorial clique where secrecy and loyalty were the supreme virtues. The regime rationalized the condemnation and purging of individuals and groups as necessary in the advance toward socialism. "Terror—against alleged class enemies, spies, and wreckers—had become

---

92   Martin, "Origins," 822.
93   Martin, *Affirmative Action Empire*, 311–12.
94   Ibid., 312.

an instrument of the state. In the Caucasus the person who wielded that instrument with brutal resolve was Lavrenti Beria."[95]

Beria, twenty years younger than Stalin, was also from Georgia. He was notorious for his ruthless determination. Among the Balkars, whether deportees or from successive generations, his name alone brings anger to the surface. They rightly associate this terrible tragedy more with him than even Stalin, as Beria was the person who authorized and encouraged vicious brutality against the nationalities.

> Beria was the central player in the chaotic era of denunciations, arrests, and cleansings of the party and state apparatus in the late 1930s, the period of the Great Purges. He was Stalin's chief henchman on the ground, first secretary of the Communist Party of Georgia from 1931 to 1938, and the virtual ruler of the Caucasus at a time when Stalin was preoccupied with [the Great Patriotic War].[96]

"The liquidation of entire villages in the Caucasus was politely referred to in letters between the two men as 'the successful fulfillment of state tasks.'"[97]

Terror became a way of life throughout the party system, as individuals had

> an incentive to denounce others before they themselves were targeted—to preserve their own positions, avenge old wrongs, and dispense with rivals while securing the gratitude and praise of superiors. Across the Soviet Union, roughly twenty-nine million people—ordinary criminals, political prisoners, peasants, and those who happened to become the target of denunciation by a boss, subordinate, or neighbor—passed through state-run labor camps or were deported en masse during the Stalin era.[98]

From 1937 to 1951, the Stalin regime systematically deported thirteen entire nationalities, totaling over 2 million people, cleansing these ethnicities from strategic border areas of the Soviet Union. The official reason for these mass expulsions was that these deported nations were inherently treasonous and disloyal to the Soviet state. The true motivation, however, was ethnic and not political, as loyal members of the Communist Party, Komsomolists (Communist Youth League), and Red Army veterans were all deported along with their ethnic kin. Active Soviet soldiers from the targeted nationalities were sent from their military station to join their nations in the special settlements as deportees. Pohl asserts that "these deportations constituted some of the most thorough cases of ethnic cleansing in world history."[99]

---

95   King, *Ghost of Freedom*, 191.
96   Ibid., 192.
97   Griffin, *Caucasus*, 93.
98   King, *Ghost of Freedom*, 193.
99   Pohl, "Stalin's Genocide," 267.

Table 1. People groups deported by the Soviet government

Nation/Nationality/Ethnic Group	Relocation Destination
Koreans	Kazakhstan, Uzbekistan
Finns, Germans	Western Siberia, Kazakhstan
Karachays, Kalmyks	Western Siberia
North Caucasus Peoples: Chechens, Ingush, Balkars	Central Asia, Kazakhstan, Kirghizia, Uzbekistan
Meskhetian Turks	Central Asia
Georgian Kurds, Khemshils (Muslim Armenians), Pontic Greeks	Central Asia, Kazakhstan, Uzbekistan, Kirghizia, Siberia
Crimean Tatars	Central Asia

In 1936 the Soviet narrative began promoting the mutual friendship between the Soviet socialist nationals and the diverse ethnic minorities within its borders. Stalin called this unique situation the "friendship of peoples" in order to unify Soviet patriotism. This friendship theme was integrated into classroom textbooks, museum exhibits, as well as countrywide celebrations.

> The textbook explained that in "no other country of the world" had there ever been "such friendship among diverse peoples as in the USSR." Significantly, this friendship did not include "foreign" nationalities; those mentioned—the Poles, Germans, Swedes, Lithuanians, and Japanese—were presented in the worst possible light, as former conquerors.[100]

At this same time, the Soviet regime was obsessed about the dangers of homeland nationalism and foreign infiltration among the diaspora nationalities already within the country. These foreign nationals were excluded from the list of Soviet nationalities and listed separately as "enemy nations," thus setting the stage for subsequent treatment of these peoples as suspect outsiders.

The deportations of earlier pre-Soviet years were undertaken primarily for security purposes. Even the deportations of the 1930s were punishment for those opposing the socialist programs. In fact the primary determinant of loyalty to the government and trustworthiness of individuals had previously been based on social standing, particularly the *kulaks*, those prosperous farmers who were able to hire help on their farms. The emerging criterion for deportation was moving from social class to ethnicity. "The measures

---

100   Hirsch, *Empire of Nations*, 291–92.

taken against the punished peoples were motivated by Moscow's—or Stalin's personal—grudges and desire to be avenged for resisting Soviet power in the interwar years."[101]

The creation of an official narrative about the transformation of the Russian Empire into the USSR was critical to the process of Soviet state-building. The Bolsheviks set out to win over the more advanced nationalities of the former Russian Empire with the promise of self-determination. However, these promises went unfulfilled. The Soviets had awakened these clans, tribes, and nationalities to new possibilities and helped them develop into socialist societies. At the same time, it had worked to eliminate the economic and cultural inequalities that had divided them in the past.

Martin described several Bolshevik conceptual categories and practices, which served as preconditions for the emergence of Soviet ethnic cleansing and were carried out as the deportation of entire nations. The first were the agricultural resettlements, which were based on ethnicity. Every nation, no matter how small, was guaranteed its own national territory, which ranged in size from five hundred people in towns designated for a specific nationality, to several hundred people in dozens of national regions and territories.

However, since not all ethnically related peoples were conveniently concentrated, ethnic consolidation became necessary, becoming the second practice of the Bolsheviks which contributed to the ultimate ethnic cleansing by the Soviets. "In some cases, it was necessary to resettle members of ethnic groups in compact agricultural settlements so they could form their own national territories—in other words, to engage in a policy of ethnic consolidation."[102] This policy, while intended to reduce ethnic conflict by satisfying national desires, in fact created an exclusive attitude leading to intolerance toward outsiders within the territories.

This led to the third practice, that of removing illegal settlers, nonnative people, from these areas which were now designated by ethnicity. "In the frenzied atmosphere of the Second World War, the Soviets again applied the same tactic that had been used in the region with cruel effectiveness almost a century earlier—the wholesale deportation of targeted ethnic groups."[103]

---

101   Yaacov Ro'i, "The Transformation of Historiography on the 'Punished Peoples,'" *History and Memory* 21, no. 2 (Fall–Winter 2009): 154.

102   Martin, "Origins," 825.

103   King, *Ghost of Freedom*, 194.

10
Predeportation:
The Massacre of Sautu

The highlanders [of the North Caucasus Mountains] knew little of Nazi phi-losophies or goals. They did have an intimate knowledge, however, of Stalinist practices. The Balkars themselves had experienced Stalinist justice a few days before the Germans arrived in the North Caucasus. On November 28, 1942, in an atrocity that remained unknown to the outside world until recently, Soviet army soldiers entered two Balkar villages with clear instructions: "Take drastic measures against the [Balkar] bandits and their accomplices. Kill them on the spot. Burn their dwellings and their possessions. Destroy everything that can give rise to future banditry. Under no circumstances is mercy to be shown." The soldiers, who were attached to the Soviet secret police, proceeded to slaughter the entire civilian population of two villages, Sautu and Glashevo, on the Cherek River, and burned two other villages, Upper Cheget and Kun-yum. An eyewitness from a neighboring village prepared a list of 323 dead, all of them old men, women, and children, as the able-bodied had been drafted to the front.[104]

Called the "secret holocaust" by villagers, it was not until 1989 that the "massacre of the Balkar villagers received public acknowledgment, when Balkar nationalists erected a commemorative memorial next to the ruins" of Sautu.[105] A small sign posted on the only road into Upper Balkaria warns:

Traveler, stop!

Honor the memory of the 470 lives of children, women and old folk

of this mountain village who were brutally shot

and then burned by the dogs of the Stalinist genocide—the NKVD troops

in November 1942.

We will save the memory of you for centuries.

From Balkaria. 1989

---

104 Karny, *Highlanders*, 357–58.
105 Ibid., 358.

We couldn't resist; we had to stop! So my friends and I drove on a nearly invisible path of grass and stone to the monument. Inscribed on a granite slab are the names of the 470 victims of Sautu.

In retaliation for the supposed assistance given to the Germans by the Balkars, the Soviet Army set out to destroy the mountain villages of the Balkars. In November 1942 the order was given to liquidate the bandits from "the villages of Upper Balkaria. Take the most decisive measures, right up to shooting on the spot, burning their buildings and property."[106] Thus the Cherek valley massacre began. Two Soviet soldiers went to a tiny hamlet of eighteen families where they "were welcomed warmly, fed and allowed to rest. In return, they warned the villagers that terrible retribution had come and that they should flee. On their return to the main force, they both admitted they had killed nobody."[107] Their commander was enraged and executed both soldiers immediately.

Photo 19: All that remains of the village of Sautu is the wall of names of those who were burned or shot on that fateful day of November 28, 1942.

Even though they had been warned of impending danger, the villagers of Sautu felt they were safe. Among their number were two former Soviet army soldiers who had been disabled in that war and sent home from the front. There were no armed men in the village.

The actual eradication of the one village, Sautu, was witnessed by at least two young children who survived the burning and executions of November 1942. Muhadin Baysiev told his story in 2010 through tears and years of heartache. He was seven years old when he saw his village go up in flames. When this author returned in 2011 to interview him a second time,

---

106   Bullough, *Fame*, 194.
107   Ibid., 195.

Muhadin was no longer capable of speaking, and has since passed away at the age of seventy-six. He had two older sisters and one younger sister who were executed along with his mother. His mother had told him to go and hide in the forest, because they would kill men, "but they would never hurt women or children."

During this time, most of the men from Sautu were fighting in the Great Patriotic War against the Germans. However, one villager was wounded in a battle with the Germans, and he was sent back to his home in Sautu. When the Soviet soldiers came to the village, he went from his home to show them his military documents. They would not even look at the documents, but executed him on the spot. One child was born in the morning, and by afternoon the Soviet soldiers had murdered the child. Muhadin, from his place of hiding, saw his mother shot, and the infant she held, though pierced with a bullet, was still alive. After the soldiers had lined up all the people and killed them, they set the entire village on fire, as Muhadin watched from the safety of the forest.[108]

Kaplan Baysiev was also a witness to this horrible situation as a twelve–year-old in the fourth grade. He also grew up in the village of Sautu and, through tears, recalled the massacre:

> One evening we heard gunshots and saw a house burning; it was connected to the mosque. People panicked and started running away from the village. Four villages were burned that same night. The Soviet Army had stayed in village homes for a special operation before the village was burned. Our father told mother to take all of the children to our grandparent's home. When we got to our grandparent's home, they had already been shot dead.
>
> Then we went to another relative's home as we were now with our mother on the street, looking for a safe place to stay. When we came to this house, one of the sons said, "We already have fifty-seven people here and we cannot take any more. We won't open the door because the soldiers are already in the village. We won't die for you." My mother begged, "How can you leave us in the street in this situation?" They finally let us in. It was a very large house and there were people in all the rooms.
>
> Then my father's brother, my uncle, came and it was already two hours into the night. He said the situation was very bad because of this burning house [next to the mosque] and it gave off such light that it seemed like day. So my uncle took us and his own children, a total of eleven people, to a cave in the mountain. He apologized that he could only take eleven people and must look

---

after his own family first. He said, "I don't know if I will have the opportunity to return for others but I must take my family first." My uncle said to let the sheep go, so they can escape and not be burned. If there was a chance the house would be burned, he hoped he could save the sheep. My uncle let the sheep out and then divided us into two groups, leading us to a mountain cave.

The son of an old woman, about 90 years old, came to give us something to eat—some dried meat and apples. We hid in the mountain cave for about one week. It was horrible and that's why all the people of this village were running away. The people were afraid because of the guns.

One night the Russian Army burned four villages in a special operation and killed many people. About 25 percent of the population was killed. When the soldiers left, we left the cave and returned to the homes that were left. There were many fires, but we put our homes back together.

To this present day, Kaplan does not know why the village was burned. "I cannot understand. I have no idea; even now, no one understands why. The official version was that some Balkarians were bandits and that was why the army did a special operation for revenge of these bandits, but I don't know."[109]

Photo 20: Kaplan Baysiev and his daughter, Zukhra Baysieva. Zukhra died during the writing of this book, and it is dedicated to her memory.

They lived in their rebuilt homes another eighteen months, until the deportation in 1944.

In Sautu, some bodies were burned to a powder and the survivors swept up the powder and buried it. Others "were buried in long trenches, since there were now too few people to bury them in proper graves."[110] On the heels of this calamity, just a few days later, German troops entered the area. They were actually Romanians, and they oversaw the remaining Balkars cleaning

109 Kaplan Baysiev, interview by the author, March 17, 2011, Upper Balkaria, Kabardino-Balkaria, tape recording.
110 Bullough, *Fame*, 203.

up from the destruction from the massacres, the fires, and the dead bodies. They even helped bury the dead.

> It did not take the Soviet army long to realize that, with a new occupier in the valley, even one as mild-mannered as these Romanians (only one German officer ever entered the Cherek valley), they had a perfect scapegoat for the crime that had been committed. The barbarity of the Red [Soviet] Army could now be blamed on the foreigners, and could be hidden for ever."[111]

The contrast between the Germans and the Soviets could not have been more striking. "Observing their religion and bearing arms were two fundamental rights the Balkars had upheld for centuries, were denied them by the Soviets, and were now fully restored by the Germans."[112]

Published documents of the deaths in Sautu range from 393 to 723. The memorial in the location of the demolished village of Sautu lists 470 victims. In the author's interviews, and in interviews by Bullough, it was clear that the villagers never believed the Soviet story that the massacres had been done by the Germans. One eyewitness interviewed by Bullough stated:

> We knew who had done this, we knew it was the Red [Soviet] Army men, and we had not expected it. How could we have expected it? If we had expected it, we would have run into the mountains. They were in Soviet uniforms, so we knew who they were. Even before the deportation [eighteen months later] these officials were saying it was the Germans who did this, but we knew they were lying all along.[113]

The betrayal by their own government, the Soviet Union, was the final insult to such tragedy.

---

111 Ibid., 203–4.
112 Karny, *Highlanders*, 358.
113 Bullough, *Fame*, 230.

11
The Deportation of the Balkars: Introduction

Awareness of the deportation of entire people groups, nations in fact, within the Soviet Union were off the world's radar screen at the time they occurred. The American government and the American people seemed generally unaware of the repressive actions of the Stalin regime against entire groups based on their ethnicity. In fact it has taken decades of information slowly leaking from within the former Soviet Union for serious study of the widespread deportation, exile, and executions of the many different people groups based on their ethnicity. "If the Caucasus occupied no major place in American strategic thinking at the beginning of the 1990s, the situation had changed decisively by the end of the decade for both positive and negative reasons." The negative reasons include the general lawlessness, the political instability, and the economic impoverishment of the region. "Russia's failure to develop a comprehensive Caucasus policy" even in the twenty-first century is an exacerbating factor.[114]

Ancient examples of the strategy of deporting conquered nations date back to biblical times when the Jewish nation of Israel was deported on two occasions to other lands in the Middle East. The first was in 722 BC when the northern portion of the land, Israel, was taken by King Shalmaneser to Assyria, a large empire of that day with its capital at Nineveh (present-day northern Iraq). The second deportation affected the southern kingdom, when the people of Judah and Jerusalem were taken captive to Babylon (located in present-day southern Iraq) by King Nebuchadnezzar in 586 BC after he had destroyed their temple in Jerusalem. Some Jews had been exiled to Babylon as early as 605 BC. However, it was following the destruction of the temple, the place of worship for the entire nation, when the majority of the Jews remaining in Judah were deported to Babylon. The deported Jews remained in exile until 538 BC when King Cyrus, who now ruled both Persia and Babylon, allowed the deportees to return to their native homeland. Of interest is the fact that King Cyrus not only allowed the Jews to return to

---

114   Paul B. Henze, "American Interest in the Caucasus," Circassian World, accessed July 15, 2011, http://www.circassianworld.com/new/north-caucasus/1167-american-interest-caucasus-henze.html.

their homeland; he also provided protection, money, and the temple articles which had been taken by King Nebuchadnezzar.[115]

The Bible records that many of the Jews chose not to return to their homeland from Persia and Babylon, as many years had elapsed since their captivity and they had become comfortable in their new habitat. In addition, most of the Jews from the ten northern tribes who were taken into captivity in regions of Assyria also never returned to Israel. These factors may help to partially explain the presence of Jews in the North Caucasus.

---

115 Ezra 1:1–5.

12
Russia's Practice of Population Relocations

From the earliest days of the Russian movement into the Caucasus, the rearrangement and relocation of populations were an essential part of the empire's political and military strategy. The burning of crops and destruction of villages were only short-term remedies, as villagers returned, rebuilt, and replanted.

> In time, Russian commanders came to understand that the complete disloca-
> tion of populations could ensure that communities conquered during one
> season did not become rebels during the next. The result was the frequent and
> substantial alteration of the demographic landscape of both the north and
> south Caucasus over the course of the nineteenth century.[116]

As early as 1854, the Tsarist officials expelled 100,000 Tatars from Crimea for their alleged assistance to Turkey during the Crimean War. From 1858 to 1865, over 500,000 mountaineers of the North Caucasus were resettled to Turkey. Estimates of the numbers of displaced mountaineers through 1878 reach as high as 2 million.

Between 1860 and 1864, military campaigns resulted in virtually emptying villages in the northwest Caucasus and along the Black Sea. Entire

> tribal groups were dispersed, resettled or killed en masse . . . [as] Russian dip-
> lomats repeatedly assured their European colleagues that the expulsions were
> not meant to be bloody and that removing the highlanders was the only way
> to extinguish banditry and organized rebellion.[117]

Stalin had deported people within the USSR when they resisted the confiscation of farms or opposed the government in others ways. Mostly these people were "relocated" to serve as cheap labor for the government, and there was a direct cause and effect. When one became an obstacle for the government, he was removed or executed. As the emerging Soviet government took over after the Tsarist regime was demolished, the young leaders of the 1917 Revolution had plans to "make Russia into a great power never again to be humiliated by the West. Their war on the countryside would forever exterminate the internal enemy, the kulaks and return the Party to the values of 1917."[118]

---

116 King, *Ghost of Freedom*, 94.
117 Ibid., 95.
118 Simon Sebag Montefiore, *Stalin: The Court of the Red Tsar* (New York: Vintage Books, 2005), 44.

In fact the Soviets had engaged in class-based deportation during the 1920s through the 1930s as a way to punish those who would dare resist the collectivization of the economy. The *kulaks*, which were considered wealthy landowners because they had increased the size of their farms to warrant hiring helpers, were the primary target. However, defining *kulak* was a question even Stalin had difficulty describing. His notes on the topic reveal that he thought of them as deserters or villagers or slaves. "The victims of collectivization included not only the wealthier peasants who employed wage labor but also vast masses of other peasants."[119] It was often left to the local military, or even the village elders, to determine who was be punished with exile. To accomplish this, the soldiers were deployed to comb the countryside, interrogate peasants, poke around in their haystacks or search their storage chests for hidden grain that had been withheld from their government-required contribution. The village elders were recruited to help in the selection of those locals who were rebellious to the cause. Since there was not a clear definition of *kulak*, locals created their own, often addressing old jealousies, such as if one farmer had been able to grow his land to require hired help. Having farmhands was considered a higher status, and under communism a hierarchy was unacceptable. As the crisis in food growth and distribution heightened, "even Stalin's staunchest lieutenants struggled to squeeze the grain out of the peasantry, especially in the Ukraine and the North Caucasus."[120] Ultimately, the term *kulak* was

> the Soviet term for the most prosperous peasants in the USSR, who exploited farm laborers. In 1929 those designated as kulaks were denounced as "class enemies," their property was confiscated, and they were sent to labor camps. Many thousands of so-called kulaks and their families died from starvation and violence.[121]

It is estimated that about three thousand Balkars and Karachay were summarily shot in the efforts to form the collectivized farms between 1929 and 1930.[122]

Buoyed by their success in improved productivity, the government in 1930 "planned the destruction of the kulaks, dividing them into three categories: First category . . . [was] to be immediately eliminated; the second to be imprisoned in camps; the third, 150,000 households, to be deported."[123] Between 5 and

---

119   Nekrich, *Punished Peoples*, 98.
120   Montefiore, *Stalin*, 47.
121   Nekrich, *Punished Peoples*, 44.
122   Robert Conquest, *The Nation Killers: The Soviet Deportation of Nationalities* (London: Macmillan, 1970), 99.
123   Montefiore, *Stalin*, 46.

7 million people ultimately fit into the three categories, meeting their fate by death squads, railway carriages, and concentration camps. During 1930 to 1931, about 1.68 million people were deported to the east, to Kazakhstan, and to the north, to Siberia.[124] By the summer of 1931, serious food shortages were then developing into a famine throughout Russia.

The Stalin regime presided over a system of national repression that dispossessed millions of people of their ancestral homelands on the basis of their ethnicity. The deported nationalities lost their birthplaces, property, much of their cultural vitality, and hundreds of thousands of lives in exile. Although deportation was not a new strategy in Russian history, it never reached such massive proportions until Stalin imposed it.

---

124   Ibid., 46, 64.

13
The Caucasus Experience: Entire Nations

There were thirteen nationalities that suffered various forms of resettlement within the Soviet Union during the later years of World War II, with a total of 3,266,340 individuals deported. These included Koreans, Finns, Germans, Kalmyks, Karachays, Chechens, Ingush, Balkars, Crimean Tatars, Pontic Greeks, Meskhetian Turks, Georgian Kurds, and Khemshils (Armenian Muslims). All of the deported nationalities consisted of peoples indigenous to the Soviet Union that had a history of conflict with the Russian Empire. The massive deportations, the movement of entire nations thousands of miles from their homelands, occurred precisely at the time Jews were being herded into death trains in Nazi-occupied Europe.

Government records of the Soviet times, as well as post-Soviet Russian officials, used a variety of words and phrases to describe the people and the actions taken against them: punished, repressed, stigmatized, collaborators (referring to the alleged collaboration with the Germans against the Soviets by the peoples of the North Caucasus), enemy nations, resettlement, enemies of the people (used against entire peoples in the prewar period and against entire ethnic groups during the deportation years), prophylactic (in the case of the Germans, intended to prevent them from potentially collaborating with the Nazi German invaders), phantom peoples, special settlers, abandoned peoples, and traitors to the homeland. In 1989 the USSR government officially declared the deported nationalities "Repressed Peoples."[125]

The peoples of the North Caucasus were some of the smallest groups to be deported, and yet these deportations involved entire nations, based solely on ethnicity. The Caucasus nationalities deported were the Karachay, Kalmyks, Chechens, Ingush, and Balkars. While all deportations were traumatic and targeted somewhat differently, depending upon the nationality, this book focuses specifically on the Balkars, who were the smallest people group to be deported.

The experiences of the deportations differ in subtle ways. For example, the Germans were subjected to a very disorganized effort, which aimed to separate the men from their families. Initially, German women who were married to

---

125   Otto Pohl, "Stalin's Genocide against the 'Repressed Peoples,'" *Journal of Genocide Research* 2, no. 2 (2000): 267.

non-German men were exempted from exile, but later deportations did not make this exemption. Additionally, Kalmyk, Meskhetian Turkish, Kurdish, and Khemshil women who were married to a different nationality than their own were exempt. However, such exemptions were not applied to North Caucasus peoples. Thus Balkar women married to other nationalities had to leave with their children, while the spouse could choose to remain, without the family, or face deportation with the family. The Balkars were the last nationality to be deported from the Caucasus, and thus the operation seemed better organized than the literature would indicate in other situations.

Many believe the USSR was largely unprepared for World War II, militarily and psychologically. The Soviets had convinced the people that their hardships were making the country the strongest in the world. An eyewitness to the madness, Aleksandr Nekrich, described the situation:

> No one—neither the people nor the government leaders—ever imagined that the war would start out so unfavorably for the USSR. The psychological preparations for the war caused people to expect not only that we would be victorious from the beginning but also that the war would be fought on enemy territory.[126]

The Great Patriotic War entered the Soviet homeland when German troops invaded on June 22, 1941. Hitler's vision of conquering the Middle East required neutralizing the Soviet forces along the way, going south through the North Caucasus region and then eastward into the South Caucasus region of Georgia and eventually to the oilfields of eastern Azerbaijan. His goal was to capture this source of oil to supply the German troops. The German occupation encountered partisan resistance to its rule over the territory from the very beginning. The Germans engaged in merciless reprisals against the Soviet citizens, killing over 2,000 prisoners of war and over 2,100 civilians. Many died of starvation, and thousands were executed by the Nazis. The conditions of the Soviet prisoners of war were inhumane and complicated by the fact "that their own government in fact repudiated them, leaving them to the mercies of fate."[127] Under the stress, torture, beatings, and indoctrination of their certain death in these prisons, some of the Soviet soldiers succumbed to the promise of a better life if they joined the German army as volunteers. This is how some of the soldiers were ultimately able to escape the Nazis and return to their own homes.

> The total number of former Soviet citizens who took up arms on the enemy side was approximately one million, which represented only 1/194th, or .5 per-

---

126   Nekrich, *Punished Peoples*, 4.
127   Ibid., 7.

cent, of the total population of the Soviet Union at the end of 1939, and only 1.75 percent of the able-bodied male population of sixteen or older. The vast majority opposed the enemy.[128]

These renegades and traitors were ultimately blamed for the deportation; those remaining to be deported were forced to pay for the treason of a small number of their countrymen.

The German push in the summer and fall of 1942 brought them within five miles of the eastern city of Vladikavkaz, on the border of Chechnya and North Ossetia. There the Germans were defeated due to overstretching their resources, making tactical errors in judgment, encountering the winter snows of the Caucasus, and facing the Soviet counteroffensive. On October 25, 1942, the Germans conquered Nalchik, the capital city of Kabardino-Balkaria Republic (KBR), where they again met strong resistance from the soldiers of the Soviet army.

When the Germans reached the North Caucasus in 1942, they set up local administrations and promoted the use of words such as "freedom," "independence," and "cooperation." The Germans offered a conciliatory hand to the Caucasus peoples, unlike the imprisonment, executions, torture, and forced labor which had been used in other places they had captured. The Germans closed the *kolkhozy* (collective farms), they reopened the mosques and churches, and they made promises of sovereignty to those people who were willing to cooperate. The Germans had been ordered to

> treat the population as friends . . . to respect private property and pay for requisitioned goods; to win the "confidence of the people" through "model conduct"; to give reasons for all harsh measures that would affect the interests of the population; and especially to respect "the honor of the women of the Caucasus."[129]

The Kabardino-Balkarian partisans were instrumental in assisting the Soviet army in recapturing Nalchik in January 1943. The people spent the next fourteen months rebuilding the economy and healing the wounds caused by the invasion and occupation of German troops, unaware that a worse fate was awaiting them. Following the German defeat in the Caucasus, the region continued to be plagued by lawlessness. The Balkars were the most resistant opponents of Soviet rule, even though they were only 12.5 percent of the population of the KBR at this point.

On August 21, 1943, the Germans took Mt. Elbrus, the highest mountain in Europe, located in Kabardino-Balkaria. Among those found

---

128 Ibid., 9.
129 Ibid., 40.

accompanying and collaborating with German armies in their advance across the southern USSR were many who were disaffected with the Soviets, including some highlanders from the Caucasus Mountain nationalities. There was a battalion composed of Soviet prisoners of war who were from the Caucasus. The Germans were also helped by North Caucasus natives who had immigrated to Europe after Russia's 1917 Revolution. Among the strategies of the Germans was the recruitment of volunteers from the peoples of the Caucasus.

The Soviet military and political leadership were in a state of confusion and chaos. The Soviet commander, Stalin, was nowhere to be found, presumably hiding in his country home. The secrecy of the Soviet government was impenetrable. "Nowhere has the invisible system of mutual cover-up and tacit understanding and the prevalence of code words and conventional formulations acquired such a sophisticated character," which impeded objective study and investigation of the atrocities committed within the Soviet Union, even into the 1970s.[130]

"Part of the population did collaborate with the Germans. There were plans to separate Balkaria from Kabarda [sic] and to unite with Karachai (on the basis of the common language and Islamic religion) under a Turkish protectorate."[131] However, an explanation of "collaborate" is necessary. When Yo'av Karny interviewed Magomed Kaygermazov, a Balkarian who was deported as a child in 1944, he asked:

> "Did you collaborate with the Germans?" . . .

> "Sure! . . . We gave them food, drink . . . We obeyed their orders . . . Who didn't? The Ukrainians did, the Belorussians did . . . But they could not be deported—there were too many of them and not enough trains. For us, a single train was sufficient. We were the scapegoats."

> He recalled the day the first Axis troops appeared in his village of Khabaz. "First came the Romanians," he recalled. "They were short and dark-haired. Only then came the Germans. They stayed three months, ate our cows whenever they felt like, and dissolved our *kolkhoz*," the Soviet-installed collective farm.

> German rule in the Caucasus lasted less than six months.[132]

The accusation of aiding the German enemy gave the Soviets the justification they used for the deportations. "The official charge was that the overwhelming majority of the deported people had collaborated with the

---

130 Ibid., 12.
131 Ibid., 62.
132 Karny, *Highlanders*, 356–57.

enemy, the Nazi army and the German occupation regime."[133] There were also some theoretical justifications advanced by Stalin himself, described by Nekrich as "the central and infallible authority of the world Communist movement on the national question and every other question."[134] There is little if any reliable documentation of treasonous activities by the North Caucasus peoples, with most of the emphasis focusing on the decrees and laws of the Soviet government related to the dissolution of the autonomous republics and their new names. The actual charges against the Balkars were decreed in a document dated April 8, 1944, one month after their deportation.

> The accusation was that during the occupation of the Kabardino-Balkar [sic] ASSR by the German fascist invaders the main mass of the Balkars had betrayed the fatherland, joined armed detachments organized by the Germans, engaged in subversive activities against Red [Soviet]Army units, assisted the Nazi occupation forces by serving them as guides in locating the mountain passes in the Caucasus, and, after the Germans had been driven out, joined bands organized by the Germans to combat the Soviet authorities.[135]

> Before the war ended, Soviet officials had become convinced that large-scale collaboration was, in fact, taking place. Such collaboration was viewed not as the fault of disloyal individuals but rather of entire, congenitally rebellious ethnic groups. Forced retaliation became the official policy for dealing with it, a tactic that had been used repeatedly—often in the same territories—by tsarist generals and Bolshevik commissars alike. In 1943 the Soviets embarked on a wave of deportation and exile, much of it overseen by Beria himself, which once again altered the demographic profile of the Caucasus.[136]

The dates are not precise because of the unavailability or unreliability of the documents of the Soviet government, but most authorities use the dates and numbers in Table 2.

"The resettlement of nationalities also had a pragmatic purpose—to colonize border regions with a 'reliable' Russian population."[137] Thus it was no accident that removing the Muslims on the borders, the Crimean Tatars on the Black Sea, and the nations of the Caucasus, also reflected tensions between Turkey and the USSR during World War II.

---

133 Nekrich, *Punished Peoples*, 90–91.
134 Ibid., 91.
135 Ibid., 92.
136 King, *Ghost of Freedom*, 196.
137 Nekrich, *Punished Peoples*, 103.

Table 2. Deportations of the North Caucasus peoples

People Group	Population Deported	Date of Deportation
Karachay	70,000	October–November, 1943
Kalmyk	93,139	1943
Chechen	300,000	February–March, 1944
Ingush	80,000	February–March, 1944
Balkars	37,000	March, 1944

The peoples of the North Caucasus were the most numerous of all the peoples deported, representing 20 percent of all the deported peoples within the Soviet Union. It is estimated that it took 40,200 freight cars to provide the transportation for the North Caucasus nations. Charles King argues that the issue is not whether the North Caucasus peoples were collaborating with the Germans. Rather the deportations exemplify a persistent Soviet policy of demographic engineering.

> According to one calculation, from 1918 to 1952, the Soviet government organized fifty-two separate relocation campaigns, removing millions of people from their homes and sending them abroad or to unfamiliar, often inhospitable, parts of their own country ... By 1949 some two million members of ethnic and religious minorities were living in deportation camps or resettlement colonies, some having been precipitously removed from their homelands and others having been born into what amounted to internal exile.[138]

As Stalin's health began failing in the early 1950s, he still had enough energy for a final purge, which included most of Beria's cronies. However, he allowed Beria himself to escape reprisal. Stalin's death in 1953 led to Nikita Khrushchev's rise to power, which in turn resulted in Beria's execution. Stalin's death also marked the end of the era of mass ethnic cleansing and genocide in the Eurasian borderlands.

Once in office, Khrushchev recanted all the reasons given for the deportations, stating that there was no military reason for the deportations. He declared that the charges "were not only absurd but grossly immoral and unjust. It is impermissible to spread public accusations of treason against every last member of a nationality, including nursing infants and their

---

138 King, *Ghost of Freedom*, 197.

mothers and helpless old people."[139] Unfortunately, this public exoneration of some of the deported peoples notwithstanding, gaining redress from the government has been elusive. "Today, all those who were publicly charged in Stalin's day with the collective commission of crimes have been exonerated, at least *pro forma*, by the government."[140] However, "in no known case have any of these victims of deportation received material compensation for the injustices which they suffered, including loss of family members and homes."[141] The Soviet government provided limited compensation to some of the deportees in the "1940s for the property that was confiscated, though the amounts were trivial in comparison to their actual losses."[142]

---

139 Nekrich, *Punished Peoples*, 94.

140 James Critchlow, *"Punished Peoples" of the Soviet Union: The Continuing Legacy of Stalin's Deportations* (New York: Human Rights Watch, 1991), 9.

141 Ibid., 10.

142 Ibid., 5.

14
Reasons Given for the Deportations

There are different perceptions of the deportations, some scholars arguing that this was a part of a continuum of pre-Soviet deportations, a strategy that has been used throughout history. Some indicate that the deportations were motivated by personal grudges and the desire for revenge against those who resisted the Soviet authority of Moscow and/or Stalin. Others claim it was a form of ethnic cleansing. Still others say it was retribution or punishment for alleged collaboration with Nazis. In 1991 the Human Rights Watch concluded that the reasons for the deportation continued to be obscure, ranging from accusations of treason and other crimes against the Soviet state, including collaboration with German invaders during World War II. In other cases, no justification was given.[143]

If there is a consistent explanation, the Human Rights Watch report continued, it appears to stem from the paranoidal fear on Stalin's part that these border regions could potentially undermine Soviet national security, or the Soviet xenophobia that Martin described.[144]

> In the mid-1930s, the criterion for determining the loyalty and trustworthiness of a person or group, and consequently for deportation or resettlement, gradually ceased being social or class, such as belonging to the category of kulak (prosperous farmer) and became primarily ethnic.[145]

Indeed peoples living on the borders of Russia were routinely resettled in the prewar period in an effort to ethnically cleanse these areas and repopulate them with trustworthy Russians. These included the Finns, Poles, Kurds, Iranians, and Koreans. These prewar deportations from the border zones were primarily aimed at "peoples who had spiritual or other ties to populations inhabiting the other side of the border and might serve as a cultural medium for the infiltration of enemy agents."[146]

Brian Glynn Williams contended that

> the real reason for the deportation may in fact lie in Stalin's plans to invade Turkey at this time. In particular, as the Red [Soviet] army moved into a collapsing Germany, Stalin contemplated the annexation . . . of the Turkish

---

143 Critchlow, *"Punished Peoples,"* 7.
144 Ibid., 8.
145 Ro'i, "Transformation of Historiography," 154.
146 Ibid., 154–55.

provinces on Turkey's northeastern border with the USSR . . . ([which] were lost to Russia during World War I).[147]

Williams asserted that as Stalin prepared for this operation (against Turkey, in which he commenced a broad propaganda campaign designed to lead to an Armenian uprising), he would also have realized that those small, distrusted ethnic groups occupied the frontier with Turkey.

> All these suspect Muslim groups were deported after having been accused of blanket treason against the . . . [motherland] during the German invasion . . . The fact that this patently innocent ethnie [the Meskhetian Turks] was chosen for group deportation lends the strongest credence to the claim that the deportation of the . . . Caucasian Muslims had more to do with Soviet foreign policy priorities than any real crimes of "universal treason" committed by these groups.[148]

This view was shared by Nekrich, who cited the fact that several Turkish emissaries visited the North Caucasus during the German occupation. Of course the peoples of Caucasus undoubtedly had no knowledge or interest in the political ambitions of Turkey.

Another plausible reason for deportation was that a small percentage of North Caucasian nationalities gave evidence of their anti-Soviet attitude. Some refused to be enlisted in the Soviet armed forces or deserted. It was indeed a sore point with the Soviets that 1.2 million from all nationalities deserted from the army and over forty-five thousand refused to be mobilized.[149]

Discontent within the republics is another possibility.

> One of the charges brought against the Balkars was that they had aspired to unite Balkaria with the Karachai [sic] Autonomous Oblast. Stalin had knowingly joined the Balkars and Kabardinians in a single autonomous unit and the Karachai and Circassians (Cherkess) in another, although the Balkars and Karachai are kindred peoples.[150]

Open disagreement with the Soviet regime was not viewed favorably.

Ultimately the Soviet government displaced people on its borders whom it distrusted, accomplishing several objectives. Removing these suspect peoples eliminated the possibility of espionage and sabotage within and across the borders; it suppressed opposition from within; it repopulated these areas with more trusted Russians; and finally, it provided a cheap supply of labor to develop the economies in the newly settled areas and contributed to the war effort.

---

147   Williams, "Hidden Ethnocide," 359.
148   Ibid.
149   Ro'i, "Transformation of Historiography," 156–57.
150   Ibid., 157.

Under Mikhail Gorbachev's policy of *glasnost* (openness), in November 1989, the

> Supreme Soviet issued a declaration ... [which] explicitly condemned the Stalin regime's deportation of eleven repressed peoples ... specifically recognizing the Koreans, Germans, Karachays, Kalmyks, Chechens, Ingush, Balkars, Crimean Tatars, Meskhetian Turks, Greeks, and Kurds as Repressed Peoples.[151]

151   Pohl, *Ethnic Cleansing*, 7.

15
March 8, 1944

By December 1932 Stalin, "satisfied that the Allies had finally promised to launch Overlord in the spring," was restored in his confidence of his own personal greatness. "When victory [over the Germans] became obvious . . . Stalin got too big for his boots and became capricious."[152] His penchant for lavish parties, drunken orgies, and unpredictable behavior resumed.

> The cost of Stalin's victories was vast: almost 26 million were dead, and another 26 million were homeless. There was a raging famine, treason among the Caucasian peoples, a Ukrainian nationalist civil war and dangerous liberalism among the Russians themselves. All these had to be solved with the traditional Bolshevik solution, Terror.[153]

With unrest throughout the country, Stalin returned to cleansing his nation of internal enemies, starting with nations in the North Caucasus, including the Kalmyks, the Chechens, the Ingush, and the Karachays. It was no accident that those deported were in sensitive borderlands with security fears of the USSR regarding Turkey. The Crimean Muslims on the Black Sea and the Caucasus Muslims represented sensitive border areas which must be secured. Nekrich concluded that while the

> deportation of peoples was regarded by the state as a preventive measure serving military needs . . . [it was also a] punitive measure . . . [and a] strategic [measure] . . . to create a more "reliable" border population. There is every reason to regard the deportations of 1943 and 1944 as a component part of Soviet foreign policy at that time.[154]

The preparations for Operation Deportation were made with great care, though their destinations were thoroughly disorganized. The entire operation was dependent on surprise and efficiency. Troops were brought in, the means of transport collected, and the routes for the truck columns established— all well in advance. Even the assignment of troops to individual families, to oversee their preparation and boarding of the trucks and trains, was determined ahead of time. Every detail was prepared in advance, including the destination and the type of work to be done by the deportees in their new destination. However, there was a total lack of attention to the human element involved in the transportation of thousands of people in cattle cars.

---

152 Montefiore, *Stalin*, 472.
153 Ibid.
154 Nekrich, *Punished Peoples*, 104.

The logistics of Operation Deportation, especially during wartime, were immense. At least 40,200 freight cars were needed. The removal of this transport equipment from military use would have been consequential. Nekrich concluded that the "consequences of the shortage of transport equipment for Soviet troops, what effect it had on the situation at the front, or how many military personnel perished because of military supplies that were not delivered in time, military equipment that was left stranded, and troops who were not redeployed in time" will perhaps never be known for certain.[155] Also impacting the war effort were the reassignment of military personnel and the diversion of fuel for Operation Deportation. Efficiency was essential to the accomplishment of the program.

The troops were trained to forestall resistance or to suppress it immediately if it broke out. The fulfillment of these aims was made easier by the fact that the bulk of the male population was absent from the territory, serving the ranks of the Red Soviet Army and in partisan units, or languishing in German captivity.[156]

There were a large number of military and security forces assigned to the Balkar deportation, "more than one member of the Soviet security organs for every two Balkars."[157] There were approximately twenty-one thousand military/security personnel assigned for approximately forty thousand Balkars!

Statistics would later show that it was women and children who bore the brunt of the punishment for betrayal and treason. When there were marriages between Balkars and other nationalities, the Balkar spouse and children were deported, while the non-Balkar spouse could remain, without their family. Nekrich reported that "not all were able to withstand this test—in some cases children were left without their mothers and husbands without their wives."[158]

The Karachays were the first of the Caucasus nations to be deported on November 2, 1943, followed by the Kalmyks in December 1943. The Chechens and Ingush were next, on the celebration day for the Red Soviet Army—February 23, 1944—when almost all of the men were at the front of the Great Patriotic War.

Having rid the Caucasus of the populations considered most antagonistic, Beria's thirst was not quenched. He turned his attention to the Balkars and on February 24, 1944, sought Stalin's approval to continue the purging of the mountain peoples, due to their alleged sabotage against the Soviet Army

---

155   Ibid., 88–89.
156   Ibid., 109.
157   Pohl, *Ethnic Cleansing*, 89.
158   Nekrich, *Punished Peoples*, 109.

on behalf of Germany. Beria's telegram to Stalin accused the Balkars of attempting to form a unified Karachay-Balkar state. Two days later he had Stalin's agreement that the entire Balkar nation deserved the punishment of deportation for alleged acts of treason. An order was issued on March 5, 1944, and three days later, on the infamous day of March 8, 1944, the Balkar deportation was carried out. This whole operation, from conception to completion, took just twelve days. The Balkars were the last of the North Caucasus peoples to be deported. After the Balkars, Stalin continued the purges, deporting the Crimean Tatars, the Meskhetian Turks, the Volga Germans, the Soviet Greeks, and others from various parts of the USSR.

For the Balkarians the deportation of an entire nation was an unthinkable event. They knew there were individuals who were disloyal to the government, but never suspected that entire families, indeed families of soldiers in the Soviet army, would be systematically punished for the acts of others. At the beginning of the Great Patriotic War five thousand Balkars joined the Soviet army. More than six hundred men from the small Balkar village of Köndelen were recorded killed in the war. The Balkars had been conquered by Russia in past centuries, and though they did not regard themselves as Russians, they accepted their fate under the Soviet government.

The day of the Balkar deportation followed the pattern of other deported nationalities: it was implemented on an important civic holiday. For the Balkars it happened on International Women's Day, an important festival in the Soviet calendar. This also coincided with the holocaust occurring in Europe. "German trains were busy transporting Jews to death camps and at almost exactly the same time that the Balkars began their journey to the east, final preparations began for the liquidation of hundreds of thousands of Hungarian Jews."[159]

By March 8, 1944, the Soviet military was entrenched in the villages and cities of Kabardino-Balkaria, and the deportation was completed with efficiency and haste. The deportation took place without notice—relying on the element of surprise to coerce the unsuspecting to obey without question. Every one of the designated nationality—men, women, the elderly, the sick, the disabled, the young—was included. The sole determination of who was to be deported from these territories was ethnicity, regardless of political loyalty. The government hunted down university students, soldiers, even decorated heroes, and other military personnel to ensure they were sent to special settlements, though not necessarily to the same settlements where their families were sent.

---

159 Karny, *Highlanders*, 360.

The NKVD [secret police] ran a dragnet through the Caucasus searching for members of these nationalities that escaped deportation in late 1943 and early 1944 . . . [and] also searched major Russian cities for members of these ethnicities and subsequently deported them . . . No geographical region under Soviet rule was safe for members of the condemned nationalities. The NKVD sought out every individual belonging to these ethnic groups wherever they sought to hide and exiled them to special settlements in desolate regions of the USSR.

The Stalin regime did not even spare Red [Soviet] Army soldiers, including officers and sergeants, Communist Party members and Komsomolists [Communist Youth League], from punishment. The Soviet government demobilized these soldiers and sent them to labor battalions or special settlements . . . without any supplies.[160]

Photo 21: Janna Bachieva (standing) with her mother Svitlana Kulbaeva.

An interesting exception was Svitlana Kulbaeva's father, who was a pilot in the Soviet Air Force during the Great Patriotic War. He learned of his family's deportation when he had one year remaining in his enlistment. He was able to continue his service to the Soviet Air Force, maintaining his loyalty to the USSR. His feeling, recalled his granddaughter, Janna Bachieva, was that "the deportation was wrong, but Hitler was also wrong, and Germany was still our country's enemy."[161]

Some of the Balkars were able to take a few possessions. Others were allowed to take nothing. Once they arrived at their destination, they were unceremoniously unloaded, as cattle, and left to fend for themselves with virtually no resources, no tools, no food, no shelter. Thousands died during the journey. An even larger number perished from hunger, cold, or disease in the forlorn places to which they were exiled. It is estimated that between one-third and one-half of the Balkar nation perished on the frosty plains of Central Asia, but "so did much of its character and heritage."[162]

The cattle cars were, of course, unheated, unhygienic, and overcrowded, teeming with typhus, tuberculosis, dystrophy, and other diseases. People died

---

160   Pohl, "Stalin's Genocide," 274–75.
161   Janna Bachieva, interview by author, March 16, 2011, Nalchik, Kabardino-Balkaria, tape recording.
162   Karny, *Highlanders*, 361.

from the sharp changes in the climate and the unbearable work, from hunger, from illnesses, from cold and malnutrition in the absence of medical care, and from nostalgia and grief over the lost members of their families.

> On arrival, the deportee groups were broken up and dispersed among remote areas of "special settlements," places in which they were kept under strict surveillance by the authorities and forbidden to leave, even to visit relatives exiled to nearby settlements elsewhere in the region.[163]

There was no infrastructure to absorb the deportees. The reception of the deportees was totally disorganized. There were few, if any, housing arrangements, let alone other community facilities. The deportees were assigned to work in agriculture, coal mining, canals, railway, industrial construction, logging, and natural gas extraction.

Apart from the unbearable living conditions to which they were subjected, especially in the first year or so after deportation, all the deported peoples had to endure further hardships that were a direct consequence of the government's policy toward them.

> The separation of the men from their womenfolk and children was an essential ingredient of this policy. Many of the men in particular were mobilized into "labor armies," which provided vast resources of cheap labor for fulfilling the production plan of a number of government commissariats (coal, oil and timber industry), and many were directed to enterprises that operated under the jurisdiction of the [government] . . . The feverish need to meet production goals meant subjecting deportees to inhuman conditions, ignoring totally the social consequences, even though the authorities were aware that the labor of deportation and camp inmates was 1.5–2 times less efficient than that of regular civilian hired labor and mortality among them was high.[164]

Brian Glynn Williams describes the conditions in the new habitation:

> Little or no preparations had been made in advance for the arrivees and most were forced to live in barracks outside factories, in dugouts, or in primitive earthen huts . . . However, most deportees who were deposited in Kazakhstan or Siberia were well-treated by the indigenous populations . . . In Siberia, many of the local inhabitants were themselves deported kulaks and political prisoners from the 1920s and 1930s; these were quick to offer assistance. Most accounts, however, stressed the hostility of the Uzbeks toward the deportees in the first year or two in Uzbekistan.[165]

In most cases the local authorities systematically encouraged an atmosphere of suspicion and hostility toward the special settlers among the

---

163 Critchlow, *"Punished Peoples,"* 8–9.
164 Ro'i, "Transformation of Historiography," 160.
165 Williams, "Hidden Ethnocide," 361.

surrounding populations. Informants were particularly helpful, for example in exposing those inclined to escape.

The Soviet government exiled the deported nationalities to areas it knew would result in mass mortality. These areas had very harsh climates compared to the homelands of the deported nationalities. They also lacked sufficient housing and food to adequately provide for the well-being of the exiles. The Balkars were abandoned in desolate areas with no shelter at all, without the aid of tools to construct primitive huts of mud. Exposure and infectious diseases were facilitated by overcrowded and unhygienic housing conditions. Malnutrition and famine-related diseases were rampant.

> Deported in the dead of winter, in the middle of a world war, without food supplies, to a strange land where no logistical measures were taken to absorb them, the Balkars and others were being led, if not into a Final solution, then definitely into a Final Dissolution.[166]

The areas to which deportees were sent had a proven track record of death for those forced to live under the special settlement regime, as the exiled *kulaks* in 1932 and 1933 had given the government all the data necessary to prove these were inhumane conditions. Yet the government did virtually nothing to improve these situations before the next wave of deportees arrived. The government forcibly mobilized many of the exiles to work in dangerous and unhealthy conditions in coal mines, logging camps, rail construction, and other forms of heavy labor, knowing this would result not only in deaths but in reduced live births.

A "welcoming committee" awaiting the deportees in Kazakhstan was described by a Balkar deportee: "An NKVD [secret police] colonel, mounted on a beautiful white horse, inspected their party and presided over a selection process. At hand were also cranky chairmen of collective farms in search of laborers."[167]

Stalin not only was the "killer of nations," so named by historian Robert Conquest, but he is also called "killer of nations' collective memories" by Yo'av Karny.

> He waged war against the Balkars' memory by banning the basic rituals of communal life: traditional wedding ceremonies were outlawed, and folk music and dancing were prohibited. The weak would die of hardships and the strong survivors, having lost access to their heritage, would cease to be Balkar.[168]

After deporting a people group, the Soviet practice was to eradicate all traces of that culture. The names of villages, rivers, roads, buildings, and hills,

---

166   Karny, *Highlanders*, 360.
167   Ibid., 359.
168   Ibid., 361.

and even the name of the provinces or republics were changed to Russian names and eliminated any reference or acknowledgment of the deported peoples. After the deportation of the Balkars, the name of the republic was changed to Kabardinian Autonomous Soviet Socialist Republic (ASSR), eliminating the Balkarians from the name.

The land formerly occupied by the Balkarians was settled by farmers from the collective farms, the *kolhozes*. After the war, efforts were made to lure new inhabitants to the vacated areas. However, the farmland, homes, gardens, and orchards had been left to ruin during the deportation. If not left to ruin, they were inhabited by others who were not of the same nationality, so the homes of the deported were no longer even available to them.

Less than six weeks after the deportation, on April 16, 1944, the newspaper of the Kabardino-Balkaria Republic, which of course had not included a word of this event, was published under a new name, completely eliminating reference to the Balkars in its title, and in its content. "Thus, the inhabitants of the republic learned that they now lived under an autonomous state structure of a different name—the Kabardinian ASSR."[169] The newspaper name itself had been changed from the *Socialist Kabardino-Balkaria* to the *Kabardinian Truth*.

In another month, on May 20, 1944, after the Balkars had already been settled in Central Asia, the newspaper was recruiting Kabardinians for higher education. It had become apparent with the deportation of the Balkars that the republic was sorely lacking in professionals of all disciplines.

> In the entire republic there were only three Kabardinian doctors. Among agronomists there was not one Kabardinian with higher education; at the large plant in Nalchik, the meat-packing complex, only one Kabardian worker was employed. In 1944 a total of only sixty-two Kabardinians completed secondary school. There were only twenty-six at the pedagogical institute [school for teachers], and the overwhelming majority of school-age children of this nationality [Kabardinian] were enrolled only up to the fifth or sixth grade.[170]

There were almost 1 million people deported through the systematic exiling of specific nations in the Caucasus and Crimea. It is remarkable that researching information on the deportation was virtually fruitless until the later part of the twentieth century. As late as the 1970s, Robert Conquest and Aleksandr Nekrich tried to write the details of the deportation and were totally frustrated at the suppression of information. Nekrich gave up his prestigious career as he endured academic isolation and, though a decorated

---

169 Nekrich, *Punished Peoples*, 63.
170 Ibid., 64.

scholar of Russia, he was persecuted for his persistence in searching for information regarding the deportations. He ultimately escaped from Moscow to America, where his work was translated into English and he gave the first account of the atrocities. "Nothing was said or written about that[the deportation of almost a million people!] anywhere! . . . You will not find a single word there [in the Soviet newspapers of 1944] about the deportation—neither in the central press nor in the local press."[171]

Robert Conquest, a British scholar, was likewise frustrated, noting that "the results [of searching for information] are extraordinary, not to say sinister, by the standards prevailing in the non-Communist world. Direct information about anything involved—even the past existence of these peoples—was, in fact, almost totally suppressed."[172]

It was as if these peoples had never even existed, as their existence, both past and present, was erased from historical documents, new editions of Soviet reference books, literary works, government statistics, and maps.

This included even works on the archeology of the regions under question, where the ancestors of the punished peoples and their cultural artifacts could no longer appear. Moreover, their archives, as well as published materials, were obliterated; they became phantom peoples.[173]

"As far as the Soviet Union was concerned, these nations did not exist" now or ever before.[174] References to them in the country's encyclopedia, maps, historical documents, and archeological memorabilia had disappeared. Graveyards and national monuments were destroyed, and the names of the collectively punished peoples were deleted from maps, streets, documents, and public memory. "They were still alive in exile, but they had ceased to exist as recognized entities."[175]

The falsification of national and regional histories was

one of the harshest legacies of the Soviet system. The consequences are momentous. The resultant ignorance fostered inadequate research and a scarcity of information on the region and its peoples. Furthermore, it has given rise to the formation of myths, the use of guesswork and the abuse of facts in the political debate.[176]

---

171 Ibid., 87.
172 Conquest, *Nation Killers*, 67.
173 Ro'i, "Transformation of Historiography," 160.
174 Bullough, *Fame*, 211.
175 Ibid., 210.
176 Helen Krag and Lars Funch, "North Caucasus: The Region, the Republics and the Peoples," Circassian World, accessed July 18, 2011, http://www.circassianworld.com/new/north-caucasus/1173-north-caucasus-region-people.html.

The Soviets not only took their property but disinherited them in another characteristically Soviet way: They blotted out the ancient Balkar names of settlements and rivers and expunged references to the past existence of a Balkar nation from the official literature. Stalin was rewriting not only history but also archaeology.[177]

The past of the deported peoples was liquidated together with their present. There was not even an official confirmation of the deportation until 1957, three years after Stalin died, and over a decade since the deportation occurred. Several of the experts have noted, with some degree of irony, the fact that in the first edition of the USSR Encyclopedia, published in 1947, the population of the Kabardinian Republic (the Balkar name had been eliminated) was made up of 60 percent Kabardinians and 10 percent Russians. There was no explanation for the fact that this did not add up to 100 percent!

The 1958 edition of the Encyclopedia corrected the math, indicating a Kabardinian population of 60 percent, with the Russians and Ukrainians making up 40 percent of the republic's population. However, there was still no mention of the Balkars. Even in the historical section, the original name of the republic, which in 1936 included the Balkars, was altered to its then-current name, excluding the Balkars. Articles published on the countries which received the deportees did not mention them by name; the closest connection is that they "live in close comradeship to other bordering nations," but it never named them.[178] It seems the Soviets were quite busy editing any books that might be consumed by the public, whether geographic, economic, or even school textbooks. In all cases, the maps and all descriptions that might bear a reference to the deported peoples were revised to make no reference at all to them, past or present. "The branding of the whole of the past life of an individual who had strayed was old Stalinist practice . . . But the application of the principle to the past of whole nations was a new refinement in the rewriting of history."[179]

After encouraging the development of the nations through the affirmative action policy of korenizatsiia (or natsionalizatsiia) throughout the 1920s, the Soviets now enforced a rigid policy of Russification and assimilation, requiring that all schools use the Russian language rather than the language of the nationalities.

The deported Balkars, however, were obstinate in "withstanding the erosion of their traditional values, especially since, in some instances at least, whole villages were deported en bloc. Even so, their ethnic culture

---

177 Karney, 361.
178 Conquest, *Nation Killers*, 77.
179 Ibid., 81–82.

and education suffered irreparable loss."[180] The children were taught Russian in schools, but were not allowed to leave their settlement for secondary or university education. Furthermore, "as late as 1952, approximately 20 percent of the children of deportees remained outside any compulsory education.[181]

> The Stalin regime embraced the ethnic prejudices of the former tsars. Despite their Georgian origins, Stalin and Beria behaved like Russian chauvinists. This marked a sharp divergence from the earlier Bolshevik policy of *koreniza-tsiia* (nativization) pursued during the 1920s and 1930s . . . which sought to promote the cultural development and political participation of non-Russian nationalities . . . These policies of *korenizatsiia* included the creation of national territorial units for national minorities supporting non-Russian cultural in-teractions, and increasing the number of non-Russians in Communist [Party] and Soviet government posts.[182]

However, these policies did not sit well with the Russian population, and their resentment of the nationalities and the special treatment they had received contributed to widespread support for the deportation policies.

The deportations during the war years, then, demonstrated a total departure from, even reversal of, Stalin's earlier adherence to internationalism, reflecting the personal attitude of Stalin and Beria toward these nationalities. Though there was some speculation that some Balkars and other North Caucasians attributed the deportation to plans to form a Greater Georgia (homeland to both Stalin and Beria), not much credibility is given this concept in the literature. Others speculate that Stalin was simply "irritated by the variety of the country's national composition, and the deportation of small peoples was intended to accelerate their assimilation into Soviet society and into large ethnic groups."[183] Again, this is in opposition to the policies Stalin promoted during the 1920s and 1930s and does not receive much attention in the literature.

The deportation of peoples did not end with World War II. Plans were underway to deport the Jews of Russia to Siberia, and it was only Stalin's death in 1953 that thwarted this plan. Greeks, Armenians, and Abkhazians were also subjected to expulsions after the war.

The first official acknowledgment of the deportations of these peoples would not dribble out until the secret speech of the new premier, Nikita Khrushchev, to the Twentieth Party Congress held February 24–25, 1956. Though it was confidential, reports began leaking in the USSR about these

---

180   Ro'i, "Transformation of Historiography," 161.
181   Ibid.
182   Pohl, *Ethnic Cleansing*, 3.
183   Ro'i, "Transformation of Historiography," 162–63.

deported peoples. The Congress also made it clear that the deported peoples "did not, so far, have the normal political rights of other Soviet nations."[184] Official action to repatriate the deportees was slow in coming.

184   Conquest, *Nation Killers*, 146.

16
Personal Experiences of the Balkars

Photo 22: Entry steps into the Balkar Museum to the Memory of the Deportees. The years of deportation are represented by each descending step.

The deportation was a sudden, tragic event that has touched thousands of victims, now reaching the fourth generation of descendants. For some it was a twist in life's journey that provided new opportunities. However, for most, it continues to be a deep scar and a bitter memory. There were a few common experiences. The deportation was a surprise in nearly every case. Even when there were rumors, people did not think it would happen to them, only to the dissenters. No one was told where or why they were going. No one expected their entire nation to be deported, only those who were being "punished." Some families were not allowed to take anything but the clothes on their backs; some families' homes were ransacked in their presence. In other cases, soldiers actually advised the families on what to take that would help in their new location. It didn't matter whether individuals were loyal Communist Party members or uninvolved professionals: every Balkarian family suffered the same consequence.

While the departure stories have different aspects, life on the trains was consistently a sordid tale. Deaths on the trains alone were "reported to have run as high as 50 percent, mainly old people, but including numerous typhus victims of all ages."[185] According to one estimate, "the total number of deaths during the journey and in the first and most difficult year of resettlement vary to some extent with the area, but most of the figures are close to two-fifths of the populations concerned, old people and children suffering the most."[186]

---

185 Ibid., 105.
186 Ibid., 107.

Though the general policy of deportation was devised by Stalin, with Beria being given charge over the implementation of the order, each village was treated according to the local military commander. In Köndelen, Boris Ulakov recounts the following:

> Four Soviet soldiers were assigned to each family. These soldiers entered the homes, scouring for gifts and valuables. Each soldier took the things he desired: some selected fabric, some leather, some clothing. My older brother, who was seven, took some fabric and hid under the table with it. As it turns out, that is the only thing we were allowed to bring on the train. No food, no clothing except what was on our bodies, and four rubles.
>
> Everyone on the train was moaning and crying. Most of the passengers were mothers, grandmothers and children. The grandfathers, and many fathers, were away at the Great Patriotic War. When the soldiers gave the signal, everyone was forced to get off the train once a day, for tea and some liquid food, and to relieve themselves. When someone died on the train, we were not allowed to bury them. The train cars were without windows and very dark. We only saw through broken places in the sides of the cars. Sometimes the soldiers opened the doors to give us air, but they stood at the doors with their rifles. The people knew absolutely nothing about what was happening. We were told the Germans were behind this, that we were punished because the Balkars helped the Germans, but that was false.[187]

Aishat Ulbasheva was allowed to bring her sewing machine, which gave her a chance to sew clothes for others in exchange for food. She was

educated as a math teacher and taught math in Kazakhstan schools; it was her duty. Now ninety years old, she described her ordeal:

> On the day before the deportation, March 7, 1944, I was working on a farm as an accountant. I was told to put the money in the safe and go home. I also put my own money in the safe with the farm's money, locked it, and went home. When I got home, I quickly saw what was going on. A soldier followed me to my home, told me what to pack, telling me the type of things I would need to bring.
>
> I was only eighteen years old. It was the prime of my life, the very best part of my life was just beginning.

Photo 23: Aishat Ulbasheva in her kitchen.

187   Ulakov, interview.

In every backyard there were five soldiers per family.

We were very poor, because all of our family's belongings had been confiscated when they started the collective farms. Our family refused to participate, so our cows and other belongings had already been taken by the government. One of the soldiers told us, "We came to deport you. You will spend a lot of time to go somewhere far away; you must take as much as you can of food and warm clothes and things you will need on your journey." We were allowed to take 15 chickens and a large bag of potatoes.

We spent an entire day waiting for a car to take us to the train station in Nalchik. When we got on the train, there were little holes in the sides of the wagon so we could see outside. However, the soldiers came with hammers and shut these little slats so we couldn't see outside.

The cattle cars that we rode in were made to carry animals, so we tried to clean the floor with our feet. Everyone was crammed into the train along with the animals some people had with them. The train was locked from the outside. There were no lights; only darkness. The only modification for human habitation was a pipe fitted in the corner for defecating.

We rode for twenty-four hours, and then the train stopped and the soldiers told us to get out. They had a tank with something liquid; I couldn't say it was food. So we ate that and some bread. We had no plates or utensils. We drank this liquid with our hands.

We were on the train for fifteen days and nights. We stopped only a few times to allow people to relieve themselves.

Everyone on our train survived. We heard that dead bodies were taken out of the cars when the trains stopped, but there were no deaths in our car. Those who died in the other cars were not allowed to be buried; they were thrown off the train by the side of the tracks.[188]

Ibrahim Gelastanov was seventeen years old when he was deported with his mother. He recalled:

Many people thought if the Germans rescued them from the Communists, life would be easier. There were a lot of people who helped the Germans during the war because many, many of the people in our village were put in jail by the Soviet government and a lot of people were suffering. The people thought the Germans had come to save them from the Communists.

Photo 24: Ibrahim Gelastanov.

---

188   Aishat Ulbasheva, interview by author, March 21, 2011, Yanikoi, Kabardino-Balkaria, tape recording.

A couple days before the deportation, I became ill and stayed home from my job at the oil factory, where we made and packed cooking oil. If I had gone to work that day, some distance from my village, I would have been sent to a different settlement than my mother.

On the day before the deportation, the military was divided so that three soldiers were assigned to each family in our village. One of the three soldiers was a counter. They came to their assigned home the day before and had a conversation with the family, checked the housing, the things in their home, how they lived. There was gossip in the village that we would be deported, so the military called a meeting of the entire village. A speaker came from the government and said no one was being deported. It was foolish talk.

At six o'clock the next morning, the order was given to leave our homes in fifteen minutes. We were awakened from our sleep by a knock at the door. Since it is not our custom to knock on doors, but rather to call out verbally, the knocking scared my mother and she did not go to the door. So they knocked harder and nearly broke the door open. So she opened it. They were very angry, and they came in with their guns pointed and demanded that we put our hands up. We were so surprised and couldn't understand what was going on. We couldn't even think about what to take. We didn't understand that it was already beginning, so the officer took a pillow cover from a pillow and started to put things in the pillow case. We thought he was taking these things for himself, but he was actually helping us. He was gathering things we would need in the place we were going, but we didn't understand.[189]

The only time Ibrahim smiled slightly was when he told about

a joke that the Americans helped with the deportation because the trucks used to transport the people from the villages to the train station were Studebakers, a part of the lend-lease program from America to assist the Soviets. Of course, we realized they were not given to the Soviet Union for the deportation, but to help with the Great Patriotic War. The Soviets used them for different purposes.

As we approached the trucks, we saw that other people were taking corn and potatoes with them. I asked the officer how we would survive, so he took us back to the house and took another pillow cover for some food for us to take. By the time we arrived at the trucks, we felt like this officer was our friend. He had helped us. All this happened in one hour, from 6 to 7 a.m.

The trains were made to carry animals, not people. There were so many people inside that you couldn't lie down; the only position you could sleep in was [he demonstrated the fetal position]. You could not even stretch out your legs because there was no space. This was our situation for fifteen days.

---

189   Ibrahim Gelastanov, interview by author, March 20, 2011, Nalchik, Kabardino-Balkaria, tape recording.

The biggest problem was to use the toilet because there were men and women together and too many people in the cars. When they stopped the train, men and women had to go together, and our people were so shamed. This especially affected the women, who burst their bladders and died. The train stopped once a day to let people off into the fields and deserts. Though many died on the trains, there were none who died in our car on the train.[190]

Photo 25: The bodies of the dead were discarded from the train during a stop. *Photo courtesy of the Balkar Museum.*

The reference to the bursting of bladders was mentioned by several of those interviewed by the author. Due to the shameful conditions, women in particular would try to restrain themselves until the train stopped each day. This condition, which is not well-documented in the medical literature, seemed quite apparent to the deportees. The Balkar Museum in Nalchik gives special commemoration to the deaths of females in this manner. The display shows a photo of the dead bodies of deportees scattered on the snow-covered ground alongside the train car. In addition, rose petals commemorating each death are strewn on the display, a stark tribute to those whose bodies simply could not deal with these inhumane conditions.

Photo 26: Usuf Olmezov in his home. Notice the Balkar images painted on the wall.

Unlike Ibrahim, who happened to be at his home when the deportation occurred, Usuf Olmezov's circumstance was the opposite. It was during the Great Patriotic War, and he was trying to enlist in the military because he was nineteen years old. The military would not enlist him, but used him as a volunteer for various duties in the mountains near his village, Kashkhatau. Sometimes he delivered documents or letters because there were no cars in the village. On the eve of the deportation, he was sent to a shepherd's house in the mountains. Several people were corralled by the soldiers and told to walk in single file in the forest or they would be shot. He continued:

---

190 Ibid.

We walked all night with many people. We kept asking the soldiers to allow us to return to our families in the village, but they wouldn't permit it. Trucks came and brought us all to Nalchik, where we were loaded on the trains. It was very difficult because when we got to the train, the cars were already full of people.

The soldiers told us we would stop once a day to relieve ourselves, and if we moved one meter [approximately three feet] away from the train, we would be shot. The elders in our train car said that when troubles such as this came, it is not a shame for men and women to do this [relieve themselves] together. We found something like a curtain, and someone had a bucket, so at least we had a little bit of privacy. It was still a shame, especially for our women, but what could you do in this situation? We were sleeping side by side in the cars.

They didn't tell us anything about where we were going or why. They gave us food once a day, and we were in the train car for fifteen days. One person died in our car, but they didn't allow us to keep him until we arrived at our destination. We had to throw him away. I couldn't tell how many people were in the car, but we were very crowded, like fish in a can.[191]

Kaplan Baysiev noted the irony of "riding on a train for fifteen days when we had never even seen a train before."[192] Boris also acknowledged the irony of his "excitement when we arrived in Kyrgyzstan, because I would be able to ride on a truck, to which someone remarked, 'He is only a child; he doesn't understand.'"[193]

There were many small villages scattered throughout the mountains of Kabardino-Balkaria, mostly inhabited by the Balkarians. By the end of the deportation period, very few of the original villages still existed. Some had been simply left to deteriorate, as was the case of Ibrahim's village. After anticipating the return to his home for thirteen years, Ibrahim returned in 1957 only to discover that it no longer existed. Voluntary repopulation efforts in many parts of the Balkarian homeland were abandoned, and most of the villages in the mountainous areas were left unpopulated. Furthermore, nearly all the homes in the lower areas were populated by the Kabardinians and Russians.

Everyone who actually endured the deportation spoke with bitterness and contempt, echoing Tolstoy's words from the previous century's attack by the Russians against the Caucasians:

It was not hatred, because they did not regard those Russian dogs as human beings; but it was such repulsion, disgust and perplexity at the senseless cruelty

---

191   Usuf Olmezov, interview by author, March 23, 2011, Kashkhatau, Kabardino-Balkaria, tape recording.

192   Kaplan Baysiev, interview by author, March 27, 2011, Upper Balkaria Village, Kabardino-Balkaria, tape recording.

193   Ulakov, interview.

of these creatures that the desire to exterminate them—like the desire to exterminate rats, poisonous spiders, or wolves—was as natural an instinct as that of self-preservation.[194]

---

194   Griffin, *Caucasus*, 100.

17
The Special Settlements

Official records show that 37,713 Balkars were deported on 14 trains to Kyrgyzstan and Kazakhstan—13,412 were relocated to Kyrgyzstan; and 18,780 to Kazakhstan; and 5,521 to Omsk Oblast in southwestern Siberia.[195] There was no serious resistance to the deportation by the Balkars; 478 anti-Soviet individuals were arrested and 288 weapons were found. The official decree listing the offenses of the Balkars included betrayal of the motherland, joining the German military, sabotage of the Soviet Army, and assisting the Germans. This alleged mass treason and terrorism had to be punished by the most severe means.

There was a range of 2,600–5,500 individuals assigned to each of the six special settlements for the Balkars in the remote wildernesses of Kazakhstan and three settlements in Kyrgyzstan. These areas were totally unprepared and incapable of adding such large numbers to their populations. In addition to the newly arrived Balkars, nearly a half million deportees had already arrived in various areas of Kazakhstan, approximately 77 percent of the North Caucasians. Most of the remaining exiles, estimated at nearly 100,000 or 22 percent, were assigned to Kyrgyzstan.

The local people receiving the deportees were ill-equipped for such an influx of foreigners. There was no infrastructure to absorb the deportees. There was virtually no housing. There were food shortages abounding throughout the entire USSR. And of course it was wartime, so military needs were the priority. All nonmilitary travel had long ago ceased. Roads and railroads had been destroyed. In Kyrgyzstan, as of September 1944, only 5,000 of 31,000 North Caucasus deportees had been provided housing. The local people were told that these special settlers were bandits, traitors, and criminals, which further isolated them and created additional hardships.

The new Balkar settlers lived under the jurisdiction of 424 Soviet officials. Most of the Balkars were assigned to agricultural work, placed on *kolhozes*, collective farms created by combining small individual farms into a cooperative where the money received and goods produced were shared among the workers based on the productivity of the farm. Others were assigned to *sovhozes*, government-operated farms created from confiscated lands. Workers on the *sovhozes* were considered employed workers and were paid specific wages. Internal passports were required for all deportees,

195 Pohl, *Ethnic Cleansing*, 90.

thus restricting them to their assigned living areas. Special permission was required by the secret police for any movement outside their designated area. The mountain-dwelling Balkars "did not adapt well to these new conditions and restrictions. The Stalin regime deliberately made their conditions in exile oppressive and punitive."[196]

During and after their physical exile, the Soviets

> sought to forcibly assimilate the surviving remnants of the "Repressed Peoples." The Stalin regime tore these nationalities from their traditional homelands, dispersed them among alien peoples, and outlawed their languages and cultures. The policy of forcibly assimilating these exiled peoples evolved throughout the late 1930s and early 1940s.[197]

By the time of the Balkar deportation, not even minimal cultural concessions were granted, unlike accomodations made to earlier deported nations.

> The Soviet government eliminated all education and publications in the native languages of the ... Balkars ... from the time of their deportation until after their release from the special settlements. Linguistic Russification of the exiles was official Soviet policy, ... [and] mandated that all children receive their primary education in Russian ... [However,] those nationalities that were indigenous to the areas of the Soviet Union they inhabited proved largely resistant to linguistic Russification. Part of this difference can be explained by the restoration of the national-territories of the North Caucasians, while the Germans, Koreans, and Greeks permanently lost their small national autonomous units.[198]

The deportees lost their rights as Soviet citizens and the native language rights they had previously enjoyed. Their children were deprived of education in their native language; they were subjected to forced assimilation or acculturation to the Russian language and culture, as opposed to the prior practice of favoring their own national culture. Less than half of school-aged children attended school, though this number was later reduced to only 20 percent. The native languages of the settlement countries were different; textbooks and supplementary material publishing had been suspended during the war, so there was nothing in their languages. There were some allowances for students to transfer to other areas in their exiled country, but they were not permitted to return to their native lands. "Despite the loss of native language schools in exile, very few North Caucasians became linguistically assimilated into either Russian or the local Turkic languages ... The North Caucasians proved remarkably resilient to assimilation."[199]

---

196   Ibid., 94.
197   Pohl, "Stalin's Genocide," 287.
198   Ibid., 288.
199   Pohl, *Ethnic Cleansing*, 95.

Cultural development of peoples came to a standstill as they focused on survival. "The desire to survive, to preserve the existence not only of oneself and one's dear ones, but of one's nation, so that someday it might be possible to return to one's native parts—this was both an unconscious instinct and a fully conscious aim."[200]

Both the actual deportation and confinement in the special settlements occurred under inhumane conditions. The deportation was greatly expedited because more than 40 percent of the exiles were children. "The Balkars in particular suffered a large number of fatalities during the deportation. Close to 3,500 Balkars (9.26 percent of the population) died *en route* to the special settlements."[201] Between 1941 and 1950, more than 377,554 exiles in the Soviet Union perished in the special settlements," nearly 12 percent of the 3,266,340 deported.[202]

The mountain-dwelling North Caucasians suffered greatly in the unfamiliar conditions of Kazakhstan and Kyrgyzstan. The climate was much more extreme than the Caucasus homeland, causing death for the people who were unprepared to cope with the severe heat and extreme cold. Many were unable to work due to lack of adequate clothing and especially the lack of shoes. Severe food shortages, scarce and inadequate housing, squalid living conditions, and lack of medicine plagued the North Caucasian exiles for years. Unheated and unsanitary housing consisted of barns, barracks, primitive structures, earthen dugouts, and makeshift huts constructed from branches. By July 1946 the authorities had only built 28 out of 1,000 planned houses to accommodate the North Caucasian special settlers in a single settlement in Kazakhstan. In another location, only 23 of 1,400 planned houses were completed. As late as the fall of 1946, many of the North Caucasian special settlers in Kyrgyzstan still lived in tents. This means that they spent the winters of 1944 and 1945 without any substantial shelter against the elements.

Food allocations were minimal, often only two hundred grams per person per day. This is less than one cup of food—about seven ounces. Marziyat Baysieva recalls her granny's story of hiding those who had died for as long as possible in order to continue to obtain their food rations.[203] These inhumane conditions led to thousands of deaths from malnutrition and other famine-related diseases; infectious diseases due to lack of hygiene and squalid living

200   Nekrich, *Punished Peoples*, 127.
201   Pohl, "Stalin's Genocide," 284.
202   Pohl, *Ethnic Cleansing*, 2.
203   Marziyat Baysieva, interview by author, March 19, 2011, Nalchik, Kabardino-Balkaria, tape recording.

conditions, including typhus, inflammation, dysentery, dystrophy, intestinal infections, yellow fever, and malaria; exposure to severe climate conditions and lack of adequate shelter and clothing; and exhaustion from the harsh working conditions, often over fourteen hours in a day. Added to this were low birth rates, which stunted the population growth among the Balkars during their time in exile. "The vast majority of deaths were the direct result of the poor physical conditions deliberately inflicted upon them by the Stalin regime."[204] And finally, there was no opportunity for people to work in the areas where they had skills, training, or experience, especially the intellectuals: writers, teachers, professors, doctors.

> The people of the special settlements lost not only their possessions and the roofs over their heads but also their fundamental civil rights as guaranteed by the Soviet constitution. They were even denied the right to an education. They did not have the opportunity to read in their own language, nor to publish or obtain literary works or periodicals in their language. Their intellectual life came to a standstill.[205]

They "lived in deplorable material conditions and had almost no rights. The Soviet government operated the special settlements as prisons without walls."[206] However, Russification was directed to those who were in schools in an effort to assimilate them to the local populations in education and culture. While some scholars have argued that their ethnic culture and education suffered irreparable loss, there was also great effort to preserve their traditions, and those traditions appear to be alive and well in today's Balkarian society. Even during the deportation, the cultural traditions were tightly held. "We kept our traditions in Kyrgyzstan, where we lived in the deportation, and if anyone broke the traditions, they were strongly criticized," emphasized Boris.[207]

It was clear that the government had no intention of the exiled Balkars returning to their homelands.

> In a secret decree from 1949, the government made clear that the exile was permanent ... By cruel coincidence, the decree was dated 26 November 1948, just [two weeks] before the Soviet Union, and all the other members of the United Nations, signed up to the Universal Declaration of Human Rights.[208]

Not only did the deportees have no right to return to their homelands; the penalty of imprisonment or hard labor for up to twenty-five years for

---

204   Pohl, "Stalin's Genocide," 285.
205   Nekrich, *Punished Peoples*, 118.
206   Pohl, *Ethnic Cleansing*, 2.
207   Ulakov, interview.
208   Bullough, *Fame*, 214–15.

violation of the rules or travel procedures were imposed. Furthermore, aiding or protecting an offender was punishable by five years of hard labor. Everyone in the special settlements, including nursing infants, was subject to monthly registration, and no one could leave their residence within a maximum number of meters without government approval. If passes were granted for travel, they had to be produced at a moment's notice. Additionally, Communist Party members who were in good standing were assigned as chiefs over groups of ten families. Every ten days they were to report regarding the state of affairs within the families. All of this, of course, was subject to the local commandant in each district, so rules were applied unevenly throughout the deportation years.

In an attempt to avoid embarrassing questions by military returning to their Caucasus homes, the government decreed that demobilized soldiers from the deported nations were barred from returning to their former homes and instructed their commanders to send them to Central Asia.

> Those former soldiers who had somehow found their own way to their former homes should be rounded up and sent to join their relatives in exile ... Even those men who shed their blood defending the Soviet Union were deemed to have betrayed it on account of their nationality.[209]

The deportees remained patriotic to the USSR, in spite of her offenses against them. "They did not rebel, there were only rare outbursts; they worked hard, ... they became exemplary workers and victors in socialist competition," more than fulfilling the quotas of their specific jobs.[210] Specifically, routine reports to Moscow on the status of deportation noted that

> in spite of this injustice [of the deportation], the Balkars demonstrated a high sense of patriotism. They joined in actively in the labor process, and the overwhelming majority of them worked honestly and conscientiously ... The Balkars labored patriotically in Kirgizia and Kazakhstan.[211]

> A new generation was growing up that had never seen the Caucasus Mountains nor the Caspian steppes nor the sea. This generation bore within itself such strong love and devotion to the land of its mothers and fathers that even if a thousand or even two thousand years went by, this longing like the force of gravity, would continue, no matter what, and all obstacles on the road home from the Diaspora would be overcome.[212]

---

209   Ibid., 215–16.
210   Nekrich, *Punished Peoples*, 128.
211   Ibid., 129.
212   Ibid., 128.

18
Balkars in the Special Settlements of Kazakhstan

Ibrahim Gelastanov continued the story of his experience when he lived in special settlements in both Kazakhstan and then Uzbekistan:

Photo 27: Ibrahim Gelastonov in his beloved Kavkaz Mountains.

A lot of people died on the trains because everyone was deported—the sick, the elderly. Young men went to the army at eighteen, so I was too young to go at seventeen years. I went to sign up, but they didn't take me. They probably already knew we would be deported.

Mother was an orphan and was forced to become the second wife to my father. Mother and I lived in one village, and father and his family lived in another village. We were separated before the deportation and then also in the new countries. Father was from my original village, and mother was from Upper Balkaria. We were totally separate. I didn't even know my father died until two years after he died. It was a horrible situation because not every family could be together in deportation, and we were divided not by the last names but by the year we were born. That is why many families were mixed, and many didn't know where their other family members were sent.

My mother and I were sent to the southern part of Kazakhstan in the Kizil Kum Desert. When our village was almost aboard the train, it happened that we couldn't fit, so we were separated not only from our family but also from our village. Father was sent also to Kazakhstan but to a different region.

The portion of southern Kazakhstan, where we were taken, bordered Uzbekistan. The last station we came to was in Uzbekistan. After we came to the railway station and got off the train, we were put on a ship and carried on a ship for two days on the Sir Darya River. After we got off the ship, there were many camels, and we put our clothes and belongings on the camels. We walked for twenty-four hours, day and night.

When we finally got to our destination, there was just a field; nothing was there. There were many families from my original village, but we had no tools to dig in the sand. We had to dig a hole for four families. Since we had no tools, we dug with our hands. All four families slept in this hole. We were like fish in a can, lying side by side. There were a lot of turtles—they came into our holes. The sand would keep falling down all around us. We couldn't build because it was sand; we couldn't even put up walls because the sand would slide down. A lot of people became sick and died because there was no food. There was no water. It was extremely hot. We couldn't even build toilets. So many people were sick. We came there at the end of March, and by the end of the summer more than half who came with us were dead.

My mother's brother was deported to western Uzbekistan. He was a good Communist, and he found us and saw us almost dying from hunger and diseases. He realized that if we stayed there much longer, we would die. So he got permission to take us to Uzbekistan where there were already some Balkars. So my mother and I were able to go to Uzbekistan in January 1945.

The war was not ended, and it was a difficult place to live. There was so much hunger; we were so hungry that I got some grass from outside. It was poisoned, but I didn't know that. Both my mom and I ate it. My mother was praying, "Lord, even if you will separate me from my body, do not allow me to separate from my faith." I still remember that prayer. She repeated it often. So she prayed that prayer, and the other prayer that she used to pray was that she would not be a bother or a burden to anyone. She died the next morning from the poisoned grass on April 20, 1945, four months after we arrived in Uzbekistan.

I was assigned to work in the cotton fields and stayed there until 1950. We were not allowed to leave the farm, not even to go to the village. But in 1950 they started gathering the young men to take them go to Tashkent, the capital of Uzbekistan, to study the minimum education to do construction work—build buildings. I knew that there was a God, and I also knew that I was a sinful person. My prayer and my dream that I asked God was that I wanted to go to town; I knew it was impossible—we were like prisoners. Then I was sent to Tashkent, and I felt this was God making it happen. They were building a KGB building, and so we were taken there as cheap hands—cheap labor—to build this new building. I was asking God to let me go to town, but I met God in town, which would have been impossible if I hadn't gotten to Tashkent.[213]

Aishat Ulbasheva's journey took her first to Kazakhstan, and then on to Kyrgyzstan.

When we arrived at our destination, there were a lot of wagons that were being pulled by cows waiting for us, along with the collective farm directors from different farms. We put all our things on the wagon, and if there was someone who couldn't walk, they would also get on the wagon. The rest of us followed the wagons by foot. There was a huge vehicle with corn dropping out of it,

213   Gelastanov, interview.

and one of the collective farm directors was picking up the corn as we walked. When we saw that, we started crying because we realized that we were coming to a place where people were hungry; he was supposed to be caring for the deportees, but he himself was hungry.

We still didn't know where we were or what we were doing. When we got to the farm building, the collective farm director looked for space for us. If anyone in the dormitory had more than one room, the room was taken and given to the new deportees. However, when the original people came from the fields, they sent their dogs after us to bite us, so we slept outside the first night. This group was comprised of half a train car load: that was about ten families for this farm, with about seven to eight people per family. There were a lot of young children.

These were sugar beet farms with a processing factory. Our job was to clear the grass and trim the area. The plants were about six inches tall. We were there to harvest them. My family stayed at this farm the entire time of the deportation.

Photo 28: Aishat Ulbasheva with her grandson, Ruslan Voronov.

When I came to that farm, they didn't know how to account for the money for the entire year. I had knowledge of this, so I helped them as an accountant. This allowed me to have some extra food, so my sisters and brothers would not be hungry. I was helping them to account, and soon I was to work for the Kazak school as a math teacher for all grades. I'm not trained to be a math teacher, but we have a proverb that "if there is no dog, even a fox can bite you." There was no one else to teach, so they used me. So I worked as a teacher, but my family worked the farm.

What was the most interesting was that my first year, there were no girls—only all boys—in my classes. I had thirty-six boys to teach.

They were so in love with education, science, and math that my watch would bother them with the ticking, so I had to put my watch outside the classroom so they wouldn't be bothered by the noise.

It was difficult with the language because even though the languages were similar, there are different endings for the words. My pupils made fun of me and laughed at me because of my use of the Kazak language. It was very difficult, and especially because of the difference in our languages. I especially had a problem because as a mathematics teacher I had to deal with all those numbers and the ends of the words were different. I remember spending the entire night preparing for lessons, and I didn't sleep at all for weeks. I couldn't spell the theorems in math in Kazak, and I spent all night practicing my pronunciation so I could give the lesson to them. Those pupils were pulling everything out of me. I was very exhausted by the end of each day.

One time a girl came to me and asked what the filling inside pies was. I didn't know! They thought as a teacher I had all the answers. If I told a child I didn't know something, I would ruin my authority as a teacher, so I couldn't say I didn't know. So I told her that it was not our topic for the day and we would discuss it at another time when we have free time. There is a time after lessons, which is called reading time (not part of the regular school course). The next day I went to schools, libraries, bookstores, looking for a book that would explain this. I did find a book to explain it, and we talked about it at reading time the next day!

We were not allowed to leave our farm, but I married someone in a different region, so I just ran away! There was a guard in charge of five families, and when I got married, I married a man in Kyrgyzstan—not only a different village but a different country! The guard over my family wrote a letter that I had run away to a different country. This letter was given to the head of the military, and then it went to the head of the region and up the military ranks. The final soldier sent it to Almaty, to the capital of Kazakhstan. So I was judged and sentenced to jail for one year for running away. They collected all the papers and sent it to the prison in my region and told the prison to arrest me and keep me in jail for one year. That prison wrote a letter to Kyrgyzstan to have me sent back to Kazakhstan. So I was just a young girl married and the military came to my home. They showed me the paper that I was guilty and I was to be in prison for one year; they had come to take me away.

My husband, an officer in the military, objected, and I was taken to a regional center. They were writing some protocol for me, and I couldn't stop myself from laughing as they did this. I don't know why, but I couldn't stop laughing as they did all the paperwork. I was laughing because I was thinking, what kind of life is this that I couldn't even get married without going to jail? It was so funny to me I couldn't stop myself from laughing. One of the soldiers was so surprised and called me a fool, and pretty soon we were all laughing. In order to go free, it was the same process backwards. The officer wrote a paper that I was innocent of any crime, as I was only following my Balkar customs. It is our custom that the bride leaves her family and goes to live with her husband's family. That paper went the same round-trip route to the prisons and military and government officials. When I was arrested, I was sent back to my family in Kazakhstan for seven months. Finally I got permission to return to my husband in Kyrgyzstan. This was in 1947. My husband continued in the military and became a famous pilot in the Soviet army, receiving many medals and awards for his service in the Great Patriotic War. I became a housewife and took care of my four boys.

I was able to return to Kazakhstan once to see my family. My husband obtained permission for me in exchange for a huge tank of corn.[214]

---

214 Ulbasheva, interview.

19
Balkars in the Special Settlements of Kyrgyzstan

Alim Kulbaev was born midway through the deportation period in 1950, the eldest of five children. By this time life was a bit normal, from his perspective. He told the story of his young years in Kyrgyzstan:

My father was sixteen when he was deported with his family. He had no professional experience, but he had trained as a shoemaker. He never got the opportunity to pursue this profession.

He was immediately assigned to the coal mine in Kyrgyzstan. I remember his face was very scary when he came home from work, as it was always black with coal dust.

My mother had also worked in the coal mine. My father noticed her and was concerned for her protection, because the coal mine was not a good place for an unmarried woman. They married in 1949 when my father was twenty-one and mother was seventeen. My family was assigned a room in a large building like a barrack, where many families lived. Living during the deportation was like a prison, because one needed permission for everything. Everyone was required to go to a registration office twice a month, and if any of the rules were broken, the penalty was twenty-five years in prison.

I remember my granny had a business on Sunday market day: she watched donkeys while the owners shopped, and I helped her. She charged one ruble, and sometimes the donkey owners gave the ruble to me.[215]

Photo 29: Mahmud Kulbaev, Alim's father, was assigned to work in the coal mines in Kyrgyzstan. *Photo courtesy of the Balkar Museum.*

---

215 Kulbaev, interview.

Usuf Olmezov described his life in the special settlements in Kazakhstan and then in Kyrgyzstan:

The train cars were very crowded, and we felt like fish in a can. One person died in our car, and we weren't allowed to keep him for a proper burial. We had to throw him away. When we got to the train station, nobody told us where we were or why we were here. The train disconnected the cars at different places and everyone was ordered to get out—maybe one car, sometimes two or three cars at a stop. Some cars went different directions. About three cars stopped at my stop. We were surrounded by fields and some salt lakes.

We went to the village and it was a village with Russian farms. We were spread to different villages and towns and farms, and then we learned that we were in Kazakhstan. There were eleven of us—all young men—who had been separated from our families.

We were told by the guards that this is the place you will live and you can choose where you want to work, either the salt mines or the farms. The guards had to leave to go back to the Caucasus, so that was the only information we had at that time. I still had not found my family.

We chose to work as shepherds for the farm cows. We divided into two groups, and one group spent all day with the cows. The other group worked in the cornfields—they followed the corn harvesters and picked up the corn that had been missed and brought home these corn droppings. We ground the corn with stones and we made a type of bread from the corn and water, and this was all the food we had. It was just eleven men—no women. We cooked for ourselves.

It was a dusty desert place. One man died and it took four days to bury him because the earth was like stone; you couldn't dig it and it was very cold. It was also a place where tornadoes came and the dust was mixed with salt because of the salt lakes. If you saw a tornado come and you didn't hide, you would die; it was guaranteed 100 percent that you would perish.

The only clothes I had were those I had worn into deportation. I had only one pair of pants and a shirt. They were my only possessions. Imagine if you must start your life in a new place with only one set of clothing—that you were wearing. I had some flea problems, and each night when I got off work, I would take off my shirt and hang it on a tree. I would take a stick from the tree and beat the shirt to have the fleas drop to the ground.

What would you think of this kind of life we had at that moment? You could not go to a different village unless the farm director gave you permission; you had to get a ticket from the military with their approval. If you did not get this ticket, they would judge you and put you in jail for twenty-five years. We tried to think why we would have such problems, but we could not think of anything. The only thing we knew was that in Nalchik the military wrote in their notebooks that we were against the Soviet Union—we were against the government, they said.

While I was there, I met a Russian woman, and she asked me to stay with her and help at her home because her husband had died. I was very happy, because she gave me his clothes and she had a shower in her home that I could use.

Staying at her home was like a paradise for me. When she died, she left her house and all her property to me. When I married a Balkar girl, I exchanged that house and all the property for one cow. After I did this, a letter came from the military. It was an invitation to me from my family who was in Kyrgyzstan. Apparently someone moved from where I lived and found my relatives. So in 1947 I was allowed to move to Kyrgyzstan and join my family there.

When I got off the train in Kyrgyzstan, I didn't know where to go or how to find the village where my relatives were. I saw a man with a military uniform and I went to ask him. At that moment he turned to me and said, "Welcome." Then he said my first and second name. I was shocked. I asked him how he knew my name. He told me that he had been at this train station waiting for me for six days. He told me my mother died but the rest of the family was okay. He was the one who sent the invitation, and he was a little angry that he had been waiting for six days. I explained to him that it took me twenty-one days to come from Kazakhstan to Kyrgyzstan because the railways were destroyed because it was wartime, so we had to detour to get here.

It was interesting because the military man at the railway station was a Chechen; it was a surprise. He was in the military and had a high rank and was in charge of the whole region, but he was also a deportee. He told me life in the village was very difficult; maybe I should stay here in town and try to bring my family here. Those who work and live in the town received tickets to get food, and for a large family there would be more food available and life would be easier than in the village. I asked what type of job I could get in the town. He offered me his influence to get me a job as a policeman. That was the most hated, despised job I could think of for me. It was also surprising because no Balkars were allowed to become police or military in that period. So I was very surprised at his offer.

I wanted to go meet my family and speak to them about this before I decided. My family of eight lived in a little room at the farm building. My father was there, though my mother had died. I saw six or seven hungry men and women and children, and I realized I couldn't help them if I lived in town. My father also advised that I not go to the town. I was happy to see my family, but on the other hand, their situation and their health was so bad that I should have cried instead of smiled. People were literally dying of starvation—they were only skin and bones. It was then that my sisters told me my mother died of starvation.

I started working on the cotton farm. Later they combined four farms and I was put in charge of all the transport by which cotton was carried into town. I remained in this village working on the cotton farms until 1957, when we could return home.[216]

---

216 Olmezov, interview.

On the train, Boris Ulakov and his mother and two brothers were mixed with some other people from Balkar villages but no one from their own village, so they didn't know anyone on the train. As a result their extended family was dispersed in several locations. His train stopped in Kyrgyzstan, and his first memory was the sight of many carts and wagons with horses or oxen pulling them. These wagons were waiting for the train passengers. He continued his recollection:

> It was raining when we arrived, so the guards gathered people and assigned them to the collective farms. There were 513 villages where Balkars were scattered. In our village, people did not suffer from hunger. There were about sixty families, but in other villages there were only ten to fifteen families. Only in our village was it tolerable. We were settled in houses that were cattle farms. In a year or two, people began to build their homes. Some didn't want to build because they thought they would soon be returned to Balkaria. The state gave each family a cow. If you wanted five heads of sheep instead of a cow, you could exchange it. Our family took five sheep, and we were given a small patch of land for a kitchen garden. We grew maize, potatoes, wheat, and other vegetables. Balkarians showed their hard work.

> They chose my father as a leader of the workers in our village. He was given a railway train to bring food rations for the deported people, so he was very serious and honest. He made a list of each family so they would get a certain amount of food. We were also able to bake bread.

> The people were to pick cotton and take care of cattle. My father received a certificate as the team leader of a village brigade. Each brigade was divided into teams, and each team leader had a certain amount of workers. Each team

Photo 30: Boris Ulakov.

> was responsible for a certain yield of cotton—35 tons/hectare [approximately two and one-half acres]. If you gave the government the required amount, you could be promoted to "hero of socialist labor." Then suddenly my father died and the doctors said he died of poisoning. My mother was only twenty-seven years old in 1945. My mother was sixteen when she married my father, who was about thirty-four. My father stole her from Upper Balkaria when she was sixteen. When my father died, my mother was pregnant with my sister, plus she had us three boys to take care of.

> Many in our village in Kyrgyzstan died of the climate. In our homeland, summer is not very hot and winter is not very cold. So the contrast in Kyrgyzstan was very difficult for our people. My mother's cousin was coming to see us,

and there had been a lot of snow. She died in the snow, and no one knew she was coming, so no one found her until spring.

We had sufficient food, as we could eat beef in the winter, as well as lamb in the spring and summer. We couldn't eat beef in the summer since there were no refrigerators, but a lamb was small enough to eat year-round. We drink *ayran* year-round. It is very good for the body.

When I finished secondary school in 1955, I learned that deported students were not allowed to enter higher education establishments. I didn't know Russian, and therefore I couldn't pass the oral and written entrance examinations. Then in 1956 Khrushchev allowed the deportees to return to their homelands and enter universities. I reapplied to the university in Kyrgyzstan, and this time I was selected to enter. I was told I could choose any program, so I selected the English department. I finished my education in Kyrgyzstan, then returned to Balkaria.[217]

Kaplan Baysiev's family was deported directly to Kyrgyzstan and lived in the same large barracks as Alim's family. When they arrived in Kyrgyzstan,

Photo 31: Kaplan Baysiev and his wife, Lyuba.

the cattle cars we were riding in were disconnected and left on the tracks at certain points along the train tracks. There were already people on the big cars with a list of people who assigned us to our living space and our new jobs. My father was assigned to the coal mine. Our family was assigned a large room, and the next morning they came and fed us and took the persons assigned to work in the coal mines—no special clothes, no training, no protective gear. Even the young boys over sixteen had to work. I was only thirteen, so I couldn't work. The children and women went into the forests to gather wood to heat their rooms. We carried large logs on our backs and received a small, dried piece of crust taken from the bird feeders. It was a time of total hunger. It was hard for everyone because it was still wartime. My mother and two of her sisters died there. This left ten children without a mother when I was fifteen years old. My father worked very hard—sometimes sixteen hours in a twenty-four-hour period. Before the deportation, my father farmed and did small administrative jobs in the village.

I was not allowed to finish my education but was assigned to the mine when I was seventeen. I lost a part of my hand in an accident at the mine in 1951,

---

217   Ulakov, interview.

when I was nineteen years old, but I continued working. What else could you do?[218]

The loss of population of the Balkars cannot be adequately measured, as the Soviets did not keep separate records for the specific nationalities. It is estimated that the Balkars suffered the same losses as other people groups due to disease, hunger, and exposure, with a loss of approximately 16 percent of the population. "Almost a third of these fatalities occurred during the transport of the Balkars to the special settlements."[219]

There is consensus among scholars that the loss was not restricted to the deported peoples. "The deportation cost the country a great deal—gigantic direct and indirect losses for the country as a whole in the long term. Cultivated land and orchards became waste. Moreover, wine-growers did not know how to sow rye or herdsmen to fell trees."[220] No matter how one considers the losses, to individuals, to families, to nationalities, to succeeding generations, or to the country, it is indeed, a terrible devastation in every regard.

218   K. Baysiev, interview.
219   Pohl, *Ethnic Cleansing*, 97–98.
220   Ro'i, "Transformation of Historiography," 159.

20
The Repatriation and Rehabilitation of the Deported Balkars

Stalin died in 1953, but it took a year until the deportees began to feel the effect. Premier Nikita Khrushchev began the de-Stalinization effort during his administration, from 1953 to 1964. In 1954 living restrictions on the deportees were lifted. Travel regulations were eased, and the monthly registration was extended to an annual requirement. Children under ten years were no longer required to register. Those over sixteen years were allowed to travel for study anywhere in the Soviet Union. Restrictions and penalties were lifted, and deportees were allowed to belong to trade unions and the Komsomol, and to obtain jobs for which they were qualified according to their education or profession. To ease the bitterness and agonies of the deportees, educational opportunities were made available, which took effect in 1955. Also in 1955, young men who were among those exiled were conscripted into the Russian army. While perhaps not considered a benefit, it was an acknowledgment that they were trusted to fight for their country.

At this same time, the deported peoples were demanding to return to their homelands after eleven years of exile. Mountaineers were leaving Central Asia, without permission, and returning to their homes, which were usually occupied by new inhabitants if they still existed. The USSR was not ready for a wholesale homecoming of thousands of dispossessed people returning to their native lands. Further, there was debate about who should be returned, as there was no consensus that all deportees should have this privilege. The pressure continued to escalate as illegal, unauthorized returns increased in frequency. Many of the deported men had served the Soviet Union in the military during the Great Patriotic War and even the 1917 Revolution; they had been party workers, partisans. "They demanded full correction of the injustice, that is, the right to return to their homeland and the restoration of their autonomous state structures."[221]

As the deportees pressed their demands on the fledgling regime of Khrushchev, there was conflict within the Communist Party leadership. The majority of members wanted to distance themselves from the policies of Stalin, but a strong minority did not want to have his legacy marred. "Only an uncompromising repudiation of the Stalin heritage and a public

---

221 Nekrich, *Punished Peoples*, 131.

condemnation of Stalinist methods and practices could strengthen the position of the Khrushchev group and provide a moral justification for its aspirations to power."[222] A compromise was reached which removed a significant portion of the deported peoples from the special register: decorated veterans of the Great Patriotic War, families of soldiers who had died in action, teachers, resettled women who had married local citizens, women of nationalities who had not been deported but who had followed their husbands into exile on the basis of marital ties, and chronically ill and disabled persons. However, the settlement did not include the families of these designated deportees, which further angered the nationalities. Additionally, the Soviet government faced a two-pronged problem with this compromise: (1) to evacuate their resettled regions would have a negative impact on the local economy, which was now accustomed to their labor; and (2) to return to their homeland was also a danger as their homes, farms, and jobs had long since been occupied by new settlers from other places within the USSR.

In February 1956 Premier Khrushchev acknowledged that "there were absolutely no military considerations necessitating the deportation of peoples, because the enemy was being rolled back everywhere under the blows of the Red Army."[223] He called the deportation of the Balkars (and certain other peoples)

> rude violations of the basic Leninist principles of the nationality policies of the Soviet Union. He emphasized the mass character of the deportations involving entire nations . . . and stress[ed] the fact that there were Communists and Komsomols [Communist Youth League] among them . . . Not only a Marxist-Leninist but also no man of common sense can grasp how it is possible to make whole nations responsible for inimical activity, including women, children, old people, Communists, and Komsomols, to use mass repression against them; and to expose them to misery and suffering for the hostile acts of individual persons or groups of persons.[224]

He alleged that these "acts were associated with the 'Stalin personality cult,' but it took eleven years (from 1956–1967) for the acknowledgment to find official, legal expression, and the wrongs that were committed may not have been fully corrected even to this day."[225]

This public condemnation of the mass repression of the Caucasus peoples was of tremendous encouragement and support to the deportees. Two months later, on April 28, 1956, the Soviet government issued a

---

222   Ibid., 131–32.
223   Ibid., 93–94.
224   Ibid., 133.
225   Ibid., 98.

decree lifting restrictions on the Balkars (among others but not all of the deported peoples), and discussion began on the repatriation process. The decree, however, explicitly prohibited those released from the settlements from returning to their homelands or receiving compensation for property confiscated during the deportation.

A bitter dispute continued among the party leadership regarding repatriating other groups, notably the Chechens and the Ingush, who were already forcing their way back to Chechnya by the thousands. The efforts of the Chechens and Ingush demonstrated that they could not be ignored, and finally, on November 24, 1956, the decree was issued, noting that previous measures had been insufficient in restoring the rights of the deportees, condemning the deportation, and restoring national autonomy, permitting their return on a voluntary basis. This was to occur for the Balkars over a two-year period, 1957–58, in order for the repatriation to take place in an organized fashion, presumably to allow time to arrange housing and jobs for the returning citizens.

Two months later, in January 1957, the reorganization of the Kabardino-Balkar ASSR was established to again include the Balkar people in the name of the republic, effective February 11, 1957. Unfortunately the legalized return of the Balkars accentuated the fact that their numbers had been significantly depleted as a result of, and during, the deportation years. The official statistics were sealed through 1978. By analyzing the "censuses of 1926, 1939, and 1970; by information on the percentages of the total Soviet population constituted by the various punished peoples; and by information on the population losses suffered by the country in general as a result of the war," Nekrich was able to put together a rough estimate of the population deterioration of the Balkar people. His conclusion indicated a net loss of a minimum of 26.5 percent of the population.[226] From 1957 to 1959 a total of 35,982 Balkars returned to KBR, of whom 14,075 were of working age.[227]

According to the 1959 census, the Balkar population was 34,088. There are many factors distorting the 1959 census, as it only reported those who had returned to their homelands, and not those who remained in the Central Asian territories of the deportation. It also did not account for the population growth of the Soviet Union as a whole, which grew about 22 percent during the period from 1939 to 1959; for the Balkars there was no growth.[228]

---

226 Ibid., 138.
227 Ibid., 141.
228 Conquest, *Nation Killers*, 169. The Human Rights Watch reported the 1959 census of Balkars at 42,208, nearly the number of Balkars that had been deported. There are often discrepancies in information obtained from the former Soviet Union.

The Human Rights Watch notes this is more than ten thousand below what it might have been in normal times.[229]

Even with its reduced population, the government-sponsored return to designated villages in the Balkarian homeland was marred by the lack of housing. The Balkars returned to their native villages only to find them in ruin, after the thirteen year abandonment, or occupied by new settlers. "Their distinctive burrow-shaped houses had collapsed, where they had not been burned by the Red Army, and were uninhabitable."[230] A government report in 1956 indicated that only 23 percent of the Balkarian homes remained intact.[231] Rather than rebuilding in their original locations, tucked away in the mountainsides, the government built straight streets with modern homes; this may have been an indication that the government wanted to maintain control of the villagers, a tactic repeated in all of the Balkar (and Karachay) valleys.

As soon as certain deported nationalities were allowed to move back to their homelands, away from the special settlements, only about 10–20 percent remained in the areas to which they had been resettled. The Balkar name was restored to its republic, again sharing it with the Kabardinians, who were not deported. In 1991 the Human Rights Watch reported that

> more than thirty years after their return, continuing suffering caused by their deportation, notably the encroachment of other nationalities during their absence, continues to delay total rehabilitation. Balkars are forced to share their autonomy with other, never-deported nationalities in what they regard as an uneven and unfair situation.[232]

Ro'i concluded that even though most of the basis for the deportation had been rescinded,

> the economic, social and political damage caused by these actions were not eliminated . . . Some of the conflicts that shook the Soviet Union under Gorbachev and its successor states in the 1990s were a direct result of the deportations . . .
>
> Altogether, the Northern Caucasus is characterized by friction between the peoples that suffered deportation and those that did not, although the deportation has not been the sole cause of their mutual animosities . . . The Balkars . . . are still smarting under the loss of much of their original land and demand full territorial redress. (In the first place, they were not allowed to return to some of their mountainous settlements; second, those parts they were able to resettle had in the meantime been occupied by Kabardinians, with whom they now had to share them.)[233]

---

229   Critchlow, *"Punished Peoples,"* 74.
230   Bullough, *Fame*, 227.
231   Ibid., 217.
232   Critchlow, *"Punished Peoples,"* 4.
233   Ro'i, "Transformation of Historiography," 165–67.

The deportation also bred lasting resentment against the central authorities in Moscow. The Human Rights Watch in 1991 outlined several steps that the Russian government could undertake to help rectify some of the wrongs of the deportation. First, it could abolish the resident permit system that restricts one's legal status to a specific location. Without express government permission, members of the punished peoples were forbidden from residing or finding work in their location of choice. Secondly, it suggested that the Russian people be informed of the innocence of these people. The literature continues to cite the assumption by the majority of Russians that the deportation was justified based on whatever reason one can conjure up. The fact is that the "rehabilitations" took place with minimal publicity, announced only in obscure official journals without mass readership. The Human Rights Watch further noted, "In no known case have any of these victims of deportation received material compensation for the injustices which they suffered, including loss of family members and homes."[234]

While deportations have been known throughout history, Ro'i asserts that

Stalin made this into a regular occurrence in order to fulfill political, social and economic assignments in the interest of the state and of "the working people." His deportations were designed to mitigate ethnic tensions in certain regions, to stabilize the political situation and to mete out punishment for collaboration with Fascist Germany. They were also intended to help gain control of uninhabited or sparsely inhabited regions and level the labor and demographic resources of the country's western and eastern parts. From the early 1930s to the early 1950s, at least six million people were forcibly resettled—some 2.5 million kulaks, and approximately 3.5 million beginning 1940. Of these six million, at least 1.2 million died during the move . . . and while they were there. Although the deported peoples contributed significantly to the development of productivity in the north and east, the costs involved in their deportation and resettlement were not covered by the property that was confiscated from them . . .

[Further,] the deportation served to accelerate their assimilation into Soviet society and into larger ethnic groups and cultures, eliminating their prospects as nations. The deportations partly obscured the genocidal aspect of Moscow's intentions and the demographic weakening of the people concerned, notably in the high mortality engendered by the forced deportation and the conditions under which they lived at the start.[235]

For some of the deported peoples, the Russification of the deportation solidified their ethnic identity as Russians. For example, the Germans,

234   Critchlow, *"Punished Peoples,"* 10.
235   Ro'i, "Transformation of Historiography," 167–68.

deported to the Gulag and special settlements, "reemerged as a unified and homogeneous ethnic group that identified itself as 'Soviet Germans' and later 'Russian Germans.' Their life experiences [during their deportation] altered their self-perception of their ethnic identity."[236] In contrast, the years the Balkars spent in special settlements far from their native lands reinforced and strengthened their national identity. Meanwhile, those who were sent to inhabit the vacated lands of the deportees accelerated the assimilation of the native peoples left behind, including the Kabardinians.

When word of returning to Kabardino-Balkaria was received in the special settlements, the reaction was mixed. Aishat Ulbasheva did not want to return, but felt no one wanted her opinion

> as a woman. I was curious regarding what happened during our absence, but I didn't want to live here. I had four boys and didn't want to go through such a move again. When my husband decided to move us, I cried all night. Kyrgyzstan was good for our family. But we were the first in our village to return in 1956. The rest of the village came two years later. But because my husband was in the military, he was able to get permission for us to return early. Even after we were set free, many people didn't know they had their freedom, and the military used that to keep a lot of people in Kyrgyzstan.[237]

Kaplan Baysiev's family returned in 1957.

> We were very happy to return. We prefer the mountain climate, which is always cool. In Kyrgyzstan, you can put an egg on the sand, and in fifteen minutes it would be cooked because of the heat. We had waited for this opportunity to return. After the Communist Party members were allowed to return, normal people returned. We never understood why we were deported. Maybe there were bandits; we don't know.[238]

Ibrahim Gelastanov was determined to return to his native village, in spite of government orders for approved areas only. His heartbreak fifty years later was evident as he viewed the empty field that had been the village of his childhood. He says:

> After Stalin died, it became easier since we had been set free and given a passport. But even though we had a passport, we could go anywhere, except back to our native village. We had to vow not to return to our native villages. I had dreamed of returning to KBR. I saw this place in my dreams, the mountains and the villages. I signed a document that I wouldn't go back to my village, but that is the first place I returned in 1956. But when I came back, there was no village. It had been destroyed and nothing remained. So I had no choice but to go to

---

236 Ibid., 168.
237 Ulbasheva, interview.
238 K. Baysiev, interview.

Nalchik where I found a job in the candy factory and lived in a dormitory. Then I wanted to go back to Uzbekistan because it was where I had the best years of my life. I missed it very much.[239]

Usuf Olmezov and his family were very happy to hear they would be able to return to their homeland. On the other hand, he continued:

I was thinking of staying two or three more years in Kyrgyzstan and then coming back later, because we had just started to get settled, to work better, to have enough food. We had finally started our new life and we had to go back. We were afraid of coming back because we didn't know if there were houses, what life would be like, what jobs we could do.

When we came back to the village, there were no houses remaining. They had deteriorated. There was just land, and someone was just about to build a home on our property. I found out it was one of our relatives, and he gave

Photo 32: Usuf Olmezov; his wife, Aziza; and their son, Arsen.

it back to me. He said if this was originally your land, I give it back to you. I started to build the house, and while we were building, we were able to rent a room for sixty rubles per month in the two-room house of a Kabardinian man.

Returning were three sisters, two brothers, and my father. Another sister and my son both died in Kyrgyzstan. My three adult daughters also live in Balkaria. My first wife died, and I remarried and have two sons.[240]

Equally heartbreaking was the return of many to their native homes, only to find that others had inhabited them as their own during the deportation years. Alim, born in Kyrgyzstan during the deportation years, had no memory of the homeland:

"Kavkaz," the Caucasus Mountains were always on the lips of my parents' generation. I didn't know what it meant, but I heard that word from an early age, and my mother explained it was her home. It was always the wish of our people to return, so when the opportunity came to return in 1957, their dream was realized and they welcomed the opportunity. My mother said, "I am ready to eat the stones and grass of my land."

239 Gelastanov, interview.
240 Olmezov, interview.

Our family returned to our father's family village, Kashkhatau, in 1957. Our home was occupied by Kabards, so the family stayed on the street the first night. We didn't really question why our home was occupied by Kabards because the government owned everything, and these people had made this home their own for nearly fifteen years. We never knew that it even still existed while we were away. You had no private property, since everything belonged to the state. It was the government's responsibility to tell us where to live, so we didn't question it. The second day the village administrator gave us one room for the family, which now included five children, two parents, and my grandmother. We lived this way for six months.

My father was able to get a loan, plus some savings from his salary in Kyrgyzstan, and was able to build a house. When we returned in 1957, there were no jobs and no salaries like we were accustomed to. Many people regretted moving back because there were no opportunities to work. So many people took jobs in Kyrgyzstan and went to their jobs for long periods of time, coming home only occasionally. My father did this for seven years.

We lived in the village until I finished high school. When I was 18 years old, the family moved to the capital of KBR, Nalchik. When we moved to Nalchik, my father was able to get a job with the state organization, building homes for families, until he retired.

Photo 33: Alim Kulbaev at his father's home.

Since I had completed high school, I tried to take the entrance examination for the university. I did not pass the exam, so I went to the military for two years. By this time I was using drugs, which I started when I was thirteen years old. I was put in prison a total of five times for drugs and stealing. I served a total of eleven years of my life in prisons or jails.

My life had a stigma on it because I was born in prison [the special settlement]. Our people were ashamed of the deportation, and we looked upon ourselves that our entire nation was considered bandits. Deportation had a big effect on my thinking. It was a stigma against one personally because you were born in prison. It was a national shame because the entire nation was called bandits. There were missed opportunities due to the deportation that didn't hinder those who had not been deported, but on the other hand, there were new opportunities and exposure to other places and cultures.[241]

241   Kulbaev, interview.

Like Alim, Svitlana Kulbaeva was born during the deportation, so the homeland was only a word in her mind. She says:

> I was seven when we left Kyrgyzstan. I remember kindergarten, and I only spoke Kyrgyz and didn't know Russian or Balkarian. My grandmother was Kabardinian and I lived with her, so that's why I didn't learn Balkarian. It was a big problem when we returned to Balkaria: school was in Russian, the village was Balkarian, and I knew only Kyrgyz.
>
> My family was happy to return, but we had a special situation: my grandmother was Kabardinian so we had family support when we returned. We were one of the first families to return. My grandmother was married to a Balkar man and chose to go with him in the deportation, but all her Kabardinian relatives remained in KBR during the deportation. We were in a better position to return than others, because we could expect the support of their relatives. We came back to their native village. Granny was not the only Kabardinian; other Kabardinians met in Kyrgyzstan and came back together.[242]

The restoration of the Balkars included the renaming of the newspaper to include the Balkar name, and the reinstating of the names of places to their original names. The Autonomous Republic was renamed Kabardino-Balkaria, to include the repatriated Balkars in the constituent republic of the Russian Federation. What could not be restored, however, were the lost opportunities. "The creation of the Balkar intelligentsia was effectively cut short. Cultural development of the Balkar people was held back because they were deprived for fourteen years of the normal attributes of a nation, its own culture, schools literature, and art."[243] When the Balkars were deported, their absence left large vacancies in the numbers of professionals and educated individuals; when they returned, their numbers had been severely reduced. Of 5,243 people in the republic with a higher education, only 74 were Balkarian; of the 6,915 in the republic with secondary education, there were only 140 Balkars. There was not a woman among these. "Five years later, in 1962, the number of Balkars who had received a higher education had increased 2.6 times, (to 193) and those with a secondary education 3.3 times (to 466), including 247 women in both categories."[244]

Those lost opportunities, those vanished years, those broken destinies, are still intensely palpable in the minds of second- and third-generation Balkars. Marziyat Baysieva's siblings benefited by parents who were so distressed by their own lack of education that it became a priority for their children. Her

---

242   Svitlana Kulbaeva, interview by author, March 24, 2011, Nalchik, Kabardino-Balkaria, tape recording.

243   Nekrich, *Punished Peoples*, 141–42.

244   Ibid., 142.

father, Kaplan, proudly exclaims that every one of his eight children has a university education, with degrees in business, journalism, management, education, textiles, and music. Two of his daughters are award-winning dressmakers of the Balkarian national costumes, elaborate and ornate works of art. His grandchildren are following that same path of obtaining higher education. Some have even been accepted into the university in Moscow, which is more prestigious than the local university.

Madina Zhanataeva and her sister, Alyona, are third-generation descendants of the deportation, and are both graduates of the university with additional graduate-level studies. Madina noted the biggest impact of the deportation on her own life is the sense of loss of national opportunity. She laments, "Our nation would be larger; there would be more cities, more opportunities, better development of our culture." Perhaps this loss explains the extreme pride the Balkars have in all things that are accomplished by their people. Twenty-two-year-old Madina continued, in excellent English:

> When I hear about famous Balkar people who speak of their heritage, I'm very proud. When someone excels in some discipline or field, it makes me proud. My favorite is poet Kaisyn Kuliyev; I like his work very much. I've memorized some of his poems. I studied about him at school and continue my interest in his biography now on my own.[245]

The defeat of Germany left the Soviet Union a leading world power despite its loss of over 20 million people during the war. However, while the Soviet Union maintained a high military profile during the postwar years,

> its citizens lived in poverty. Between 1964 and 1985 a series of reactionary leaders did little to relieve the suffering of the Russian and Soviet peoples. Khrushchev was ousted in 1964, and Leonid Ilyich Brezhnev took power. His rule was marked by growing economic problems and unrest in the non-Russian republics . . . Most of Russia's people lived in conditions little better than those in the poorer countries of Africa.[246]

In 1985 Mikhail Gorbachev became president of the USSR, creating

> internal reforms such as *glasnost* (openness) and *perestroika* (restructuring and reform) [that] led to profound changes within the Soviet Union as Moscow's iron grip weakened. By 1989 ethnically based national movements demanding greater autonomy had emerged in most of the union republics. Within the Russian Federation, non-Russian nationalities also called for greater freedom from Russian domination.[247]

---

245   Zhanataeva, interview.
246   James Minahan, *Miniature Empires: A Historical Dictionary of the Newly Independent States* (Westport, CT: Greenwood Press, 1998), 232.
247   Ibid., 232–33.

As the Soviet Empire began to disintegrate in the late 1980s, the Caucasus was one of its first regions to experience serious disorder and degeneration. Since the disappearance of the Soviet system at the end of 1991, no part of the Caucasus has been free of armed conflict, economic deterioration, or political turmoil and confusion.[248]

In 1989 Mikhail Gorbachev issued an official acknowledgment from the government condemning the deportations, calling them "barbaric acts" and contrary to international law. Gorbachev's acknowledgment of the horrors of the past empowered the Balkars to erect a monument memorializing those massacred and place it on the ruins of Sautu.

In June 1991 Boris Yeltsin became the first democratically elected Russian president. He disbanded the Communist Party, and an attempted coup forced the resignation of its head, Gorbachev, in August 1991. Yeltsin began recognizing the independence of Russia's nations, setting the pattern for liberating a number of ethnic nations from the Russian Federation over the next several months. This led to the rapid disintegration of the Soviet empire and the creation of the most decentralized state in Russia's long history. The new Russian Federation was now a "multinational state of over 128 recognized national groups."[249]

"Before its collapse, the Soviet Union finally formally repudiated the Stalinist policy of national deportations, almost 40 years after Stalin's death."[250] With the new Russian constitution of December 1993, these republics lost much of their specific status and were transformed into administrative units on a par with other regions. They are known formally as subjects of the Russian Federation.

On July 31, 1992, a public admittance that the murders in the four Balkar villages had been committed by Soviet troops was announced, and the regional parliament of Kabardino-Balkaria officially declared that the massacres in Upper Balkaria were an act of genocide.

In 1994, on the fiftieth anniversary of the deportation, Boris Yeltsin marked the occasion by issuing a solemn decree in which he proclaimed, "The Balkars drank to the full from the cup of humiliation. I bow my head in memory of the dead."[251] He assured the Balkars that they would receive justice for the inhumanities to their nation. He was the first Russian official who publicly apologized to the Balkar people for the deportation.

When asked their reaction to Yeltsin's apology to the Balkars, some had

---

248 Henze, "Russia and the Caucasus."
249 Minahan, *Miniature Empires*, 234.
250 Pohl, *Ethnic Cleansing*, 7.
251 Karny, *Highlanders*, 367.

not even heard of it. Svitlana Kulbaeva felt it was a good thing, because it might change the impression of others that "we were some sort of criminals, so returning us, rehabilitating us to our land, returning our good name, our reputation—these are all good things."[252] Aishat Ulbasheva agreed, stating, "I was very happy. It touched my heart."[253] Others felt Yeltsin's apology was only for political purposes and changed nothing for the Balkars.

Yeltsin's policies became increasingly unpopular, and on December 31, 1999, he announced his resignation and installed his chosen successor, Vladimir Putin, as president. Putin worked to centralize authority, using the rationale of protecting civil society from terrorism. The "regime's drive to centralize power and authority has been pursued with a shrewd relentlessness but has complicated the matter of relations among communal groups, albeit probably unintentionally."[254]

This intensified centralization of power has been accompanied by increased and extended terrorist activities in the North Caucasus. The greatest tragedy was at the elementary school in Beslan, North Ossetia, in September 2004 when

Photo 34: This is one of the walls in the gymnasium of Beslan School #1, where over three hundred children and adults were incinerated in 2004. The gunshot holes remain in the wall where photos of those killed are posted.

one thousand hostages were taken and over three hundred children and adults were killed. The terrorist violence in Nalchik, Kabardino-Balkaria's capital, in October 2005 resulted in sixty deaths. Officially the Putin administration categorized these conflicts as part of the Global War on Terror.

In a very interesting article by Gerber and Mendelson, they note that the tolerance of the Russian population for casualties in ethnic conflicts reflects similarly to the US responses. "Concern over casualties has remained

---

252 S. Kulbaeva, interview.

253 Ulbasheva, interview.

254 James Warhola, "Religion and Politics under the Putin Administration: Accommodation and Confrontation within 'Managed Pluralism,'" *Journal of Church and State* 49 (Winter 2007): 88.

by far the most predominant sentiment in regard to Chechnya," with the Russian people growing less tolerant over time. Clearly, the argument of the importance of containing Chechen violence as a part of the war on global terrorism was not convincing to the Russian population.[255]

Ultimately Warhola considers that "far from contributing to the unity and stability of the country, the policies resulting from the general centralization orientation of the Putin regime has had a fracturing effect."[256] Both the government policies and the general socioeconomic conditions contribute to the continuing tensions in the North Caucasus region. Gerber and Mendelsōn go a step further in asserting that the government's response to the Chechen uprising in 1999 "fomented ethnic intolerance . . . fostered terrorism, undermined civil liberties within Russia, and jeopardized the stability of the Caucasus region."[257]

Only one survivor of the Stalin Terror has pursued compensation through the courts. In October 2002 this survivor, who was six years old at the time of the Sautu massacre, took her case to the courts. They agreed that a specific action, rather than a mass action like the deportation itself, had occurred, and awarded compensation for it. However, the compensation for the loss of her father, her family, and all their possessions, and a delay of sixty years, was the equivalent of two months' salary. Only one other survivor chose to pursue legal justice. "As for the other survivors of the massacre . . . they treated the state with the contempt with which it had treated them and ignored it."[258]

In order for a potential breakup of the Kabardino-Balkar Republic, civil strife between the Kabardinians and the Balkars would be necessary. Although there are tensions between the two peoples, it seems that the ethnic hostility required does not exist, as both nationalities have learned to live together.[259] Arutiunov agrees, noting the friendly relations between the Kabardinians and Balkars, with numerous mixed marriages, workplace relationships, and the mixed population of many of the villages.[260]

Marziyat Baysieva is a remarkable example, as she not only married outside her faith, Islam, but she married outside her culture, to a Jewish man. When asked whether her family was more upset with her for marrying outside her ethnicity or outside her religion, she gave an astonishingly

---

255 Theodore P. Gerber and Sarah E. Mendelson, "Casualty Sensitivity in a Post-Soviet Context: Russian Views of the Second Chechen War, 2001–2004," *Political Science Quarterly* 123, no. 1 (2001): 48.

256 Warhola, "Religion and Politics," 88–89.

257 Gerber and Mendelson, "Casualty Sensitivity," 40.

258 Bullough, *Fame*, 225.

259 Karny, *Highlanders*, 368.

260 Arutiunov, "Ethnicity in the Caucasus."

insightful answer: "If my husband had made an effort to please my relatives, perhaps they would have become softer toward him. But he didn't do that, because he didn't care about my family or my relatives."[261]

The repatriation and rehabilitation of the peoples to their homelands was intended by the Soviet Union "to encourage the fusion of the nationalities into a single Soviet people. In reality, the Soviet experience made the political units of the Caucasus considerably less ethnically diverse and more clearly national than they had been in the past."[262] However, it also continued to cause friction between the peoples who had suffered deportation and those who had remained. For the Balkars, there is continued resentment over the loss of their original land (the mountainous areas that had deteriorated and where they were not permitted to return); having to share their original space with the Kabardinians who settled in these lands during their deportation; and most critically, the continuing resentment against Moscow, which had orchestrated these moves.

---

261 Baysieva, interview.
262 King, *Ghost of Freedom*, 206.

21
The Lingering Effect of the Deportation on the Successor Generations

The deportation of 1944 had a profound psychological effect not only on the deportees, but also on the remaining nationalities, including the Russians, who lived in the vacated regions. "The forced expulsions also produced what would become one of the region's epic stories of oppression under Russian rule, with generations of [the deported victims] eulogizing their exile as a national tragedy."[263] Indeed the deportation is on the lips of those directly affected even in the first meeting with strangers. It is a tragedy of epic proportions in the minds of those who experienced the deportation, and they can recall the images quite clearly even in their elder years.

> The relatively small number of the Balkars seems to have helped them be one of the first deported nationalities to be substantially relocated to their homeland. However, the returnees found their homes and farms pillaged and in a state of destruction; only a few places had been spared.[264]

Before the deportation the Balkars raised 40 percent of the livestock in Kabardino-Balkaria, but now

> they have "lost" this profession because their pasturage has not been returned ... Moreover, the Balkars have difficulty in finding other employment ... not a single industrial enterprise has been built at a Balkar population point, even though deposits of raw materials ... in the mountains are on traditional Balkar land.[265]

Having heard about the deportation from early childhood, successive generations feel the pain of their forefathers deeply. They also mourn the losses—of opportunity, of education, of destiny, of their native homes. As Svitlana Kulbaeva put it, "Our entire generation was delayed."[266]

> It is generally agreed among Russian—and other—historians that the deportations were a loss economically, not only in respect of the regions concerned,

---

263   Charles King and Rajan Menon, "Prisoners of the Caucasus," *Foreign Affairs* 89, no. 4 (July–August 2010): 23.
264   Critchlow, *"Punished Peoples,"* 74.
265   Ibid., 75.
266   S. Kulbaeva, interview.

but of the country as a whole. Differences,
however, exist regarding views of their political
motivation and the long-term political and
social significance and implications of the
repression of these "enemy nations"... Some
insist that the deportations, while inflict-
ing terrible material and spiritual hardship,
had the effect of consolidating the punished
peoples and constructing or remodeling their
ethnic identity.[267]

Social

In addition to securing the borders of the
USSR, the deportation also provided the Soviet
government with a source of labor to develop

Photo 35: Svitlana Kulbaeva.

the infrastructure, mining, agriculture, and industry of Siberia, Kazakhstan,
and Central Asia. Using this labor force developed the largely untapped
economic potential of the interior of the Soviet Union. However, the Russian
Federation continues to reap the harvest of social problems directly related to
the deportation of these peoples. President Dmitry Medvedev has pointed to
unemployment and corruption in the North Caucasus "as the chief sources
of instability."[268]

Unemployment in Kabardino-Balkaria is highest among the Balkars,
who also happen to be the primary inhabitants of the mountainous regions,
where commerce, manufacturing, and industry do not exist. The highlands
are best suited to agricultural endeavors, but without adequate land even
these efforts are thwarted.

In an interesting article articulating an opposing theme, Arutiunov
argues that

> the highland pasture lands owned by many Balkars have allowed for the
> extensive development of sheep and Angora goats, and the processing of wool
> and knitwear. The result is that Balkar income is about 10%–20% higher on
> average than Kabardin income.[269]

The North Caucasus has been closed to foreigners until recently. Some
of this region had well-developed tourist resorts and spas which attracted
visitors from all over the Soviet Union. They are now largely deserted due
to the overall economic situation, to armed conflicts in the region, and to

267   Ro'i, "Transformation of Historiography," 169–70.
268   King and Menon, "Prisoners of the Caucasus," 24.
269   Arutiunov, "Ethnicity in the Caucasus."

general anti-Caucasian sentiment among Russians. In the absence of social stability, tourism cannot be revived.

> The Caucasus region has a pleasant climate rich in natural beauty, plenty of historical relics, exotic customs, ancient architecture, etc.—everything needed for a successful tourist industry. What it lacks is social stability. Tourism requires security, suppression of crime and terrorism, a decent and effective police force, and so on.[270]

However, this will require not only stability of the social and political environment, but a change in attitudes. Caucasians are generally unwilling to work in tourist jobs, considering them servile, while Russians will not work for non-Russian bosses; thus, for the tourism sector to flourish, "there must be significant changes in both social interaction and national mentalities."[271]

Karny's interview with Kaygermazov provides a peek into the mindset of Balkars when it comes to forgiveness. After providing detailed insight into the horrors of the deportation and life in the settlements, Kaygermazov was asked what he thought of the Soviet regime after Stalin's death.

He responded without hesitation. "Much better than the present 'democracy'. . . I wish Stalin could rise from the dead and restore law and order." He continued to defend Stalin. As Karny suggested that Stalin's "law and order" had not quite benefited the Balkars, the highlander offered a resolute defense of the dead dictator. "He did not know, he did not see the decree . . . He was manipulated."[272]

Karny cites other Balkar deportation survivors with similar responses, and sums it up with an observation by Balkar historian Svetlana Akiyaeva: "Forgiveness is imbedded in our character."[273]

Eleven years later in 2011, this author's interview with Svitlana Kulbaeva, who was born during the deportation in Kyrgyzstan, produced a similar response. Svitlana recalls that at Stalin's death "everyone was crying. It showed that Balkars were in the mainstream of the country; since everyone else was crying, Balkars mourned too."[274]

Karny argues that the memory of the deportation is becoming a distant past for the current generation. He tells stories of interviews with individuals who experienced the deportation as children and who now refuse to share this painful experience with their grandchildren. He asserts that the

---

270 Ibid.
271 Ibid.
272 Karny, *Highlanders*, 361.
273 Ibid., 362.
274 S. Kulbaeva, interview.

rare human species of the Caucasus may be gone in just a few decades with only scant attention paid to their plight by the outside world. A very small number of those who survived with their memory intact have been trying to rescue the past, but they may be too late.[275]

Political

A major complaint of the Balkars is that there are few Balkars in the upper levels of their republic's administration. Although there were funds allocated to assist the Balkars in rebuilding their national existence, individuals have never received compensation for their suffering at the hands of the state. It is estimated that

> 85 percent of the funds allocated under the rehabilitation decree never reached their intended destination . . . [but were diverted for use in the Kabardinian areas]. In seventy-five years of Kabardino-Balkaria's existence, not one factory has been constructed in our mountainous regions, and 98 percent of the highlanders are unemployed.[276]

Some attribute the problems in the North Caucasus to the deportation. Certainly the lack of industrialization and land disbursement has taken a toll on the opportunities to provide a livelihood for the Balkars. Based on work by Arutiunov, the conflicts that have erupted in the North Caucasus, and specifically in the Kabardino-Balkaria Republic, are usually "ethnically disguised economic conflicts, triggered by social and economic uncertainty, redistribution of property, struggle for key positions, etc."[277] Arutiunov asserts that there are two factors which have combined to play an important role in providing continuity and social order in Kabardino-Balkaria. The first is that the government functionaries are former Communist Party members. This has provided continuity in governing the republic and in dealing with Moscow. Secondly, recognizing the importance of informal power structures and the role that personal networks continue to play has a great influence on maintaining the social order. These personal influencers have more weight than even the formal governmental structures; the village elders command more respect than government officials.

> These mechanisms are most effective in traditionally oriented societies and economies. Unfortunately, in many societies in the northern Caucasus today, a large number of young men are growing up without exposure to or respect for traditional values. As such, there is a danger that new conflict is growing

---

275   Karny, *Highlanders*, xxv.
276   Ibid., 367–68.
277   Arutiunov, "Ethnicity in the Caucasus."

in the region. If there is to be any chance of avoiding this, it must be through economic development.[278]

Violence and instability have increased dramatically throughout Russia, but most significantly in the North Caucasus. Often the violence is alleged to be initiated by people from the North Caucasus and escalated by the police and military. In 2002, when security forces attempted to rescue hostages in a Moscow theater, over 170 were killed. Dozens were killed in suicide bombings in and around Moscow from 2003 to 2004. On September 1, 2004, over one thousand teachers, children, parents, and siblings came to Beslan School #1 in neighboring republic, Ossetia, to celebrate the first day of classes. A bomb thrown into the school turned it into an incinerator as over three hundred teachers, parents, school children, and their siblings were killed in the fire. In 2004 two Russian passenger airplanes were brought down by suicide terrorists. In Nalchik, KBR's capital, 145 were killed when terrorists attacked security forces in 2005. A high-speed train was derailed by a bomb, killing thirty passengers, as it traveled between Moscow and St. Petersburg in 2009.

None of this equals the higher level of violence that regularly occurs in the North Caucasus, labeled the "epicenter of routine political violence in the country."[279] The increase in terrorist activities in the North Caucasus has alarmed the Russian government, for so long the heavy-handed controller of criminal activities in this country. In 1997 there were thirty-two acts of terrorism, and this increased steadily to over five hundred in 2003.[280] The area has seen terrorist crime increase by 60 percent in 2009 compared to 2008; the government noted that "80 percent of all terrorist incidents in Russia take place in this one small slice of land," the North Caucasus. In October 2009 President Medvedev told Russia's Security Council that the North Caucasus remains the "country's foremost internal political problem,"[281] as the terrorism previously confined to Chechnya was spreading to neighboring republics.

In early 2010, Medvedev, in response to nearly a decade of unrest among the Caucasian peoples, some of which has spilled over to Moscow and other areas of the country, created a new North Caucasus Federal District with jurisdiction over six of the seven republics in the North Caucasus region, a sort of "super republic." He installed a businessman who is considered an effective and tough administrator. This appointment "essentially re-created an old imperial post that disappeared with the advent of the Bolsheviks:

---

278 Ibid.
279 King and Menon, "Prisoners of the Caucasus," 20.
280 Warhola, "Religion and Politics," 76–77.
281 King and Menon, "Prisoners of the Caucasus," 21.

viceroy of the Caucasus."[282] However, the insurgent activities in Kabardino-Balkaria have continued unabated. In 2010 there were 108 attacks against law enforcement personnel, including judges and prosecutors, in which forty-two were killed. Additionally, thirty-one civilians were killed and fifty-three injured in attacks. In January 2011 the KBR president, Arsen Kanokov, called the prognosis for the crime situation "disappointing."[283]

In February 2011 three Russian tourists were murdered in the ski resort area of Mt. Elbrus in the Kabardino-Balkaria Republic. This resulted in counterterrorism restrictions being imposed in the villages and portions of Nalchik. There were additional checkpoints put into place, and a 9 p.m. curfew was imposed in the villages, limiting the movements of citizens.

The influence of Islam on the violence is unclear. Some are quick to blame religious fervor as the underlying cause; others blame the economic conditions facing the region, and in particular the Balkars.

The Islamic insurgency is, however, becoming increasingly active. Since April 2010 the Kabardino-Balkar-Karachay *jamaat* (Islamic community) has systematically gunned down dozens of police, security officials, and government officials (past and present); set up roadside booby traps; and improvised explosive devices. In February 2011 the republic's government called on citizens to close ranks to combat the "terrorist threat" and has also asked Moscow to help stabilize the situation.[284]

The counterterrorism restrictions were lifted in November 2011 as the government declared "that the Kabardino-Balkar-Karachai wing of the North Caucasus insurgency has been weakened to the point that it no longer poses a threat."[285] However, insurgency leaders in Kabardino-Balkaria have posted clips on their websites affirming that, though they have lost many of their colleagues, "there is no shortage of new volunteers, and they remain wholeheartedly committed to the jihad."[286] Perhaps militants from outside the area, or even outside of Russia, have had influence on the Islamic efforts in the past, but these insurgency leaders assert, "Today the local *jamaat*

---

282   Ibid., 24.

283   Mairbek Vatchagaev, "Rebel Attacks in Kabardino-Balkaria Skyrocket," *Eurasia Daily Monitor*, February 4, 2011, 1.

284   Liz Fuller, "Kabardino-Balkaria Authorities at a Loss How to Cope with Militant Threat," Radio Free Europe / Radio Liberty, February 16, 2011, accessed February 17, 2011, http://www.rferl.org/content/kabardino-balkaria_at_loss_on_militant_threat/2311663.html.

285   Liz Fuller, "Counterterror Restrictions Lifted in Kabardino-Balkaria as Insurgency Again Gathers Strength," http://www.rferl.org/content/kabardino_balkaria_insurgency_ north_caucasus_counterterrorism/24388125.html (accessed November 30, 2011).

286   Ibid.

in Kabardino-Balkaria does not require any outside help."[287] They have organized *jamaat* structures in all the major towns in the northwest Caucasus. Of interest to note is that those involved in the Kabardino-Balkaria *jamaat* are young, with most under thirty years of age, and none over forty. Their primary motivation seems to be resistance against any secular government as they seek to impose sharia law, and the nature of the attacks becomes more targeted, more sophisticated, more aggressive, and more violent.

The Moscow government has been unable to fix the underlying problems of economic development and governance, as payoffs of local officials and deployment of the state's substantial repressive apparatus are no longer effective. King and Menon predict:

> If the Kremlin cannot contain the cycle of attacks and counterattacks, then Russia's nationalist groups—many of which spew chauvinistic rhetoric de-monizing Russian non-Christian minorities—could gain traction in Russian politics ... A new upsurge in violence within and beyond the North Caucasus would also accelerate Russia's drift away from democracy, by providing fodder for politicians who promise to avenge the victims and hammer the disorderly south ... The government may invoke public safety to justify the further re-striction of civil liberties and concentration of power inside the Kremlin. Both outcomes—increased nationalism and increased authoritarianism—would, in turn, hamper progress on arms control and make cooperation with the West on issues such as energy, Iran, and North Korea even more difficult.[288]

There have been several interethnic crises between the Balkars and the Kabardinians, as each has moved toward self-determination. President Kokov ruled authoritatively from 1992 until 2005. He won each election with overwhelming majorities, with little if any opposition. The Balkars, in many cases, boycotted the voting process in protest. His rule was one of the most authoritative in Russia, as he resisted democratization efforts from Moscow. Moscow seemed to ignore his resistance since he brought a semblance of stability to the republic. "KBR was one of the most authoritarian of the Muslim republics, consistently near the bottom in rankings of Russia's regions."[289] Indeed, as the Islamist threat has turned to the KBR from neighboring republics, Kokov was overly aggressive in the suppression of Muslims, giving him a reputation as a repressive puppet of Putin.[290]

---

287 Vatchagaev, "Rebel Attacks," 1.
288 King and Menon, "Prisoners of the Caucasus," 21.
289 Gordon M. Hahn, "The Rise of Islamist Extremism in Kabardino-Balkariya," *Demokratizatsiya* 13, no. 4 (Fall 2005): 554.
290 Ibid., 559, 562.

Cultural

As for cultural matters, there are at present no native-language schools, but this is apparently not a burning issue, since Balkar parents had themselves requested Russian instruction for their children. The Balkars are said to accept the idea of bilingualism (as reflected in the fact that nearly four-fifths are fluent in Russian, one of the highest rankings in the 1989 census), but there is apparently now a movement to re-establish native-language schools. The Balkars have a newspaper in their own language, *Zaman*, and a national theater dance company which recently won first prize at an international competition in Turkey . . . There is radio and television broadcasting in Balkar, and a publishing house in the capital city of Nalchik which publishes books in Kabardinian, Balkar and Russian languages.[291]

Photo 36: Balkarian dancers have won international acclaim.

The Balkarians celebrate one national Balkar holiday, the Rebirth of the Balkar Nation, on March 28. This date was declared in 1989 to commemorate the return of the Balkarians from their special settlements. Since it is their national holiday, Balkarians do not work on this date, but rather attend meetings with ceremonies and dignitaries to honor their reunification. In the villages, cows are often sacrificed, and there is a celebration with food, friends, and families.

The fierce commitment of today's young people to their Balkarian traditions is evidence that these have been instilled into their consciousness more than any other thing. Commitment to marriage within the nationality, respect for elders, loyalty to parents, and pride in their nation are signs that the traditions will not be easily wiped away.

Spiritual

While 90 percent of those who claim Islam as their faith do not attend mosques, their self-identification as Muslims is the factor that is considered in estimating the population. Throughout all of Russia, the ratio of Russian Orthodox adherents to self-identified Muslim adherents in 1926 was 16:1; by 1999, after seventy years of atheism taught by communism, the ratio had switched to 10:1 in favor of Muslims. In KBR the Muslim population is 70 percent, and is

---

291   Critchlow, *"Punished Peoples,"* 76.

growing numerically as well as by percentages. Religious solidarity is limited, as the Muslims are relatively weakly connected communities.[292]

Malashenko believes that the revival of Islam has been initiated by "changes in the consciousness of Muslim people, such that the religion component is increasingly more important . . . [Forty-eight percent of the Balkarians believe that Islam] should define all spheres of social life."[293]

Before 1917 there were twelve thousand Muslim communities and mosques throughout Russia; in 2004 there were 3,537 registered—16.3 percent of the total number of religious communities. Officials estimate that the numbers are much larger.

In 2006 the Orthodox Church recommended that in addition to the Orthodox courses taught in the public schools, also "the 'Basics of Muslim Culture'. . . be taught by Muslim clerics in the North Caucasus region."[294] This was an attempt by the Orthodox Church to maintain its own influence in an increasingly pluralistic society.

Scholars agree that at the heart of the Islamic separatist movements in the North Caucasus

> lie strong nationalist sentiment, distrust of the Russian Government, and a poor (or worsening) economic outlook . . . Putin's anti-federalist policies, which have given much more power to the Russian federal government at the expense of individual Russian states/regions [have fueled Islamic separatism].[295]

Islam is penetrating other activities throughout Russia, including the establishment of a bank which follows the Islamic practice of not charging a percentage on banking transactions. Islam is influencing the insurance business; encouraging the increased production and sale of *halal* products (products which have been produced according to Islamic standards); and inspiring new shops selling religious articles, literature, and Islamic clothing.

Educationally, few of the functioning mosques have clergy who have completed higher education. In the 1990s young men seeking Islamic education went to Arab countries, Turkey or Pakistan; however, the Islamic teachings were based on Arabic cultural traditions, and this created divisions among the North Caucasus Muslim community. As of 1998 there were 108 registered Islamic secondary educational institutions. In 2006 slightly over two hundred students were enrolled in the Higher Islamic College in

---

292   Alexei V. Malashenko, "Islam in Russia," *Social Research* 76, no. 1 (Spring 2009): 321–22.

293   Ibid., 324–25.

294   Warhola, "Religion and Politics," 83.

295   Charles Bartles, "*Russia's Islamic Threat:* Book Review," *Military Review* 87, no. 6 (November–December 2007): 120.

Moscow.[296] It has been difficult to build a unified educational system due to differences among the Muslims. Secondly, accreditation has been denied by the Russian government as there is still distrust of Islamic education, so graduates cannot be awarded diplomas, either in religious or secular subjects.

The traditional Muslim groups have sought government sanction of their affairs, from the establishment of the clerics' salaries to the examination of the clerics. As a result the KBR Muslim hierarchy

> inspected the ranks of local Muslim clerics, . . . examining the nature and extent of the [local] Muslim clerics' knowledge of Islam to weed out and better compete with extremists. Nearly one hundred imams in the KBR were forced to undergo retraining regarding their knowledge of Islamic theology and law . . . In another [examination], eighty-seven of one hundred and fifty of the village imams failed to demonstrate proper knowledge of Mohammed's teachings, interpretation of the Koran and knowledge for the performance of Islamic rites.[297]

Nekrich contended that the deportation

> brought to a halt the struggle for atheism, reversed the decline in religious fanaticism and preserved the influence of the Islamic religion and sects, and considerably strengthened the influence of religion. And what, after all, could the deported peoples turn to, if not religion? . . . Cultural and educational work came to a complete stop—there were no newspapers, no books, and no motion pictures in the native languages. All this created exceptionally favorable conditions for the increased influence of religion, an influence which historically had been to a certain extent both anti-Russian and anti-Soviet.[298]

Griffin agreed that Islam is best when practiced against something, namely Russia. It then becomes the most cohesive representation of pride and thirst for nationalism.[299]

While religious institutions and activities were either suppressed or tightly controlled during the Soviet years, the spiritual life of the Balkarians appears to be influenced mostly by the family, with traditions preempting all other influences. Some see the deportation as being influential because of the different locations and opportunities to engage in religious experiences that might not otherwise have been available to them. Others acknowledge their dependence on prayer, without acknowledging a specific religious philosophy or deity. And, for those who have lived in the distant shadow of the deportation, they claim no influence of the deportation on their

---

296 Malashenko, "Islam in Russia," 30.
297 Hahn, "Rise of Islamist Extremism," 566.
298 Nekrich, *Punished Peoples*, 155.
299 Griffin, *Caucasus*, 227.

spirituality. Ultimately, Gordon Hahn asserts that "the ethnic cleavage seems to supersede the confessional in the KBR's intercommunal politics."[300]

The growing Islamization of initially secular ethnic movements and the failure of the government to respond adequately pose a significant problem for the Russian government. Research has shown that the disparity between rich and poor regions have an influence on the role of religion in society, especially "in the KBR, which is one of Russia's poorest regions."[301]

> During the Soviet period, religion did not play an important role in society, at least not overtly. But it has always been an integral part of the peoples' identity. Today the impact of religion as a factor of distinction is on the increase in the North Caucasus. It is also used for articulating ethnic identity on the political scene. This notwithstanding, it must be pointed out explicitly, that conflicts in the North Caucasus are not religious conflicts. Religion is an integrated factor of the cultures, yet does not form the basis for hostility between groups, even though the media, particularly Western media, regularly describe them as Christian-Muslim conflicts.[302]

> Kabardino-Balkaria has been, historically, a Muslim—specifically Sunni Muslim—region. Most people there today call themselves Muslim, but they mean vastly different things by this label. Some focus on moral law, others on political identification, still others on the poetry and mysticism of sacred texts. The Soviet period effectively wiped out a great deal of the theological expertise on Islam. But this purge never managed to affect deep moral codes . . . Religion is complex in Kabardino-Balkaria; being a seeker there is a highly dynamic affair.[303]

In the mid-1980s, there were less than ten mosques in three of the North Caucasus republics: Adygea, Karachay-Cherkessia, and Kabardino-Balkaria. By 2001 there were ninety-six mosques in KBR alone. Nearly every village boasts its own mosque, or at least an Islamic community center. In 1993 the first Islamic Institute, funded by Saudi Arabian money, began to train young men for the Islamic clergy. Additionally, about "one hundred KBR students were studying abroad in Saudi Arabia, Egypt, Syria, Jordan, and Turkey."[304] In addition to the public, registered religious communities, there are an estimated "forty Islamic communities across the KBR, encompassing more than ten thousand followers."[305] These are the foundation for recruiting young men.

---

300   Hahn, "Rise of Islamist Extremism," 553.
301   Ibid., 547.
302   Krag and Funch, "North Caucasus."
303   Margaret Paxson, "They Call It Home," *Wilson Quarterly* (Spring 2009): 36.
304   Hahn, "Rise of Islamist Extremism," 548.
305   Ibid., 568.

Indeed some believe that "Balkar nationalism could more readily be converted into Islamic nationalism, given the minority and outsider status of this small Muslim ethnic group in the republic" and its generally more impoverished population.[306]

> Unemployment among Balkars, especially in the republic's mountainous regions, is as high as 80–90 percent in some areas, creating an environment on which criminality and radicalism can feed . . . In the village of Köndelen alone, with its population of 6000, 99 percent of working-age adults are unemployed and surviving on subsistence farming.[307]

> Renewed spiritual interest in Islam is especially apparent among the youth in the Caucasus since the collapse of the Soviet Union. [They are the primary attendees at the mosques, ranging in age from fourteen to thirty-five.] Their parents look on their religious children with interest and sometimes a measure of puzzlement, wondering what this new devotion will mean. What are young people looking for? Order where there has been chaos in their lives? Holiness where there has been transgression? Belonging where there has been estrangement?[308]

Hahn concluded that

> the cultural divide between the predominantly secular and increasingly decadent postmodern Russian culture and even traditional "official" Islam in Russia, . . . is further alienating Muslim believers from the predominantly secular Russian society . . . Russia's embrace of postmodernism's sexual and other forms of nihilism (particularly by the elite's privileged offspring) is contributing to the Islamist backlash among Muslims in the KBR.[309]

> The western republics [of the North Caucasus] have taken a much more secularized attitude to religious rituals and symbols to date. Their Muslim identity is predominantly cultural . . . Few of the peoples are religious in a traditional ritual sense, and most remember, live or revive traditions from a pre-Christian and pre-Muslim period. The traditions live alongside each other in a non-antagonistic fashion . . . Rituals and holidays [are generally] locally based, often very much alike for Christian, Muslims and Jews and with clear roots in history. Syncretism of pagan and different religious rituals are more the rule than the exception. Pagan traditions are also upheld as proof of ancient rights to the region.[310]

An interesting observation on the nonantagonistic nature of the religions in the North Caucasus is revealed as Nalchik, the capital of Kabardino-

---

306   Ibid., 577.
307   Ibid., 554, 571.
308   Paxson, "Home," 36.
309   Hahn, "Rise of Islamist Extremism," 549.
310   Krag and Funch, "North Caucasus."

Balkaria, is the center of the Jewish community in the Caucasus, the location of the area's largest mosque, and home to several Christian fellowships. While still in the special settlement in Uzbekistan, Ibrahim Gelastanov knew he was searching for a God that must exist. He thought that if he got to a larger city, he would find God.

> I knew there was a God and I knew I was a sinful person. I prayed that God would allow me to go to Tashkent, the capital of Uzbekistan, to learn a trade. And then I was sent to Tashkent, and I felt this was God making it happen. I asked God to allow me to go to the town, and I met God in town. This would have been impossible if I had not gotten to Tashkent.

> At the end of 1952 I met a Ukrainian man, and I learned that he was a believer in Jesus. He invited me to attend church with him, but I was afraid to go. I didn't know what kind of church meeting this was, and I was afraid it might be criminal. I really wanted to go, but I was afraid. In June 1953, after continuing my friendship with this man, I did go to the church. There were about one hundred people, many who sat on the ground outside the building because there was not enough room inside. I was thinking that if God is one, if there is one God, there can only be one way to Him. I didn't consider myself a Muslim, but I was searching for the way to God, whether it would be Islam or Christianity. Everyone was very friendly, and I thought I was in heaven. I thought everyone there was holy and I was the only sinner. It touched my heart very deeply. Since we were under Communist rule, they could not ask people to repent or preach a sermon, because that was considered spreading religion. At the end of the summer I asked God for forgiveness, and I was so happy I could not contain myself.[311]

Ibrahim was a member of the Communist Youth League. It was 1953 and Stalin had died.

> The Komsomol officials were trying to discourage me from church activities, promising a beautiful vision of the communal future. Meanwhile the church officials were encouraging me to be baptized as a Christian, so I faced a dilemma. When I returned to Nalchik, as my village in the mountains had been destroyed, I found a gathering of Christians and was baptized.[312]

Ibrahim Gelastanov was the first Balkarian to become a Christian. Because of his linguistic

Photo 37: Ibrahim Gelastanov, holding the Bible that he translated into the Balkar language.

---

311   Gelastanov, interview.
312   Ibid.

abilities, he has been the pioneer in translating the Bible from Russian into the Balkarian language. At the time of this writing, there are only a few books remaining to be translated into his native tongue. Ibrahim attributes his becoming a Christian to the deportation, because "only by those trials and difficulties could I come to Jesus. If there was no deportation, I would have followed my family's tradition and continued the path to become a good Communist."[313] His choice of words is of interest, as the alternative to Christianity was communism, not Islam. Ibrahim remained the only Balkar Christian until 1989, when a second Balkar man chose to follow Christ.

Usuf attributes his family's experience to God's protection, though he does not restrict himself to a specific religious tradition. He said:

> I think the deportation took place only because God allowed it to happen. If you went through such difficulties as we did, you would think of God more often than ordinary people. I think that it was predestined that we would have sorrow, that we would be deported. And the fact that we returned—God is also in charge of that too, so we must stay strong in our faith regardless of what happens.[314]

As often happens when people go through trouble, it can either turn them to God or away from Him. Usuf continued:

> We became closer to God because we had been praying to God all the time to keep us from the worse things that were happening. We realized how poor our situation was, but we kept praying to God to keep us from worse things. A lot of people doubted God, asking, "Why did you bring this upon us?" But I was always asking God not to allow things to get worse. I think that my prayer was answered, because when we were deported, the soldiers did not expect us to return. They didn't think of sending us back. We were just moved to the new country. The fact that we came back is only by the grace of God. If He didn't help us, I would have just perished in the desert. My family was very happy and praising God that we could see each other and that He allowed us to become a family again. The entire event was God's blessing after a twenty-one-day trip on the train and finding the guard waiting for me. It was all God; not a specific thing, but the entire event.[315]

Among first-generation descendants of the deportation, spiritual issues seem to have been more influenced by the communist teaching of atheism in the schools rather than imparted by parents. Alim Kulbaev was born in 1950, midway through the deportation years. Life had taken on a new normal as his Balkarian family lived in a special settlement in Kyrgyzstan. He said:

---

313 Ibid.
314 Olmezov, interview.
315 Ibid.

Our grandparents taught us prayers, and we accepted atheist teaching from the schools. We were taught to believe in Lenin. Such things in our culture were accepted as spiritual; there was no difference between literature and the needs of the soul. Balkarians are mainly atheist; it is all about their traditions, but not related to faith. It is deep in their heart for Balkarians to be atheist. Children accept the concept that there is no God since they are taught that in school. Traditions in our culture are much more powerful than Islam. Everyone in the village lives close together, and your behavior to get along in society is most important. Islamists are trying to break these traditions because these traditions keep us together as a society.[316]

Alim found himself in jail several times due to drugs and various related crimes. The fifth time he was incarcerated, he was married with two small children. During this time in prison, Alim met Ibrahim, the first Balkar Christian. Ibrahim gave Alim a copy of the New Testament in 1990. Alim continued his remarkable story of redemption:

> I began reading the New Testament with interest because my life seemed so hopeless. I had failed with it, and I could see that clearly. I was old enough to see that there was no chance to change anything in my life, and so there was nothing to live for. I simply wanted to die. However, I had a slight hope that the Almighty might help me to get out of this mess.

> In 1992, after I got out of jail, I again met Ibrahim on the street, and he invited me to come to church. I went. It was a baptismal service. I was so convicted in my sins that I decided to go directly forward and accept Jesus as my Savior. I realized that I would not live without Him any longer.

> Then, like that demon-possessed man, I heard God's call: "Return home and tell how much God has done for you." I obeyed it, and people who knew me were amazed. Many of them confessed that Jesus is the real God if He could change a person like me.[317]

Photo 38: Alim Kulbaev and his wife, Haulot.

In 1992 Alim Kulbaev became the third Balkar Christian. He later attended the North Caucasus Bible Institute and began pastoring a small Balkar congregation.

Marziyat Baysieva, the daughter of Kaplan, was amazed at the power of her grandmother's faith. She was astonished that through all the trials and difficulties

316 Kulbaev, interview.
317 Ibid.

of her granny's life as a deportee, her grandmother still thanked God for taking her through those hard times. She shared her memory:

It is interesting how kind most of this [deported] generation is, with soft, open hearts. I remember many times the poor came begging for food or money, and she would always invite them in and serve them tea. Some even slept in our bed. She would never say no to anyone who needed help.

Those of Granny's generation were deeply religious; they were always praying to God, no matter how difficult and painful life was. My own generation is so far from God, and yet the elderly keep praying, even to this day. Though the government pressed them to reject their faith, they kept their faith through it all. I cannot say the same for my generation. The interesting thing also is that Granny's generation was open to anyone—Muslim, Christian, alcoholic, drug addict. But in my generation there are so many aggressive people who try to divide people into different groups in order to reject them. It looks like they search for a reason to start arguing about their differences.

My father's dream was for his children to have the education he was deprived of. The deportation has left a deep scar in his soul. Even now, whenever we buy something, like food, he says we shouldn't buy so much. He was so afraid that even now he keeps thinking it could happen again. He has a fear all these years that these things might be repeated. Even now, if he sees homeless or orphaned children on television, he will start crying because he remembers being in the same position, and it is clear that all these memories are still with him. He has not forgotten these sufferings.

Photo 39: Marziyat Baysieva, a second-generation Balkar.

The only reason that I could think of why blessings came to our home was because Granny was always praying and thanking and praising God. That is the reason God gave us a family again, with eight children in my family. Granny continued to pray until she died.[318]

During the Soviet years, religion was prohibited and atheism was the replacement which was taught in the schools. God may be taken out of the marketplace, but He does not vacate the hearts of people. As the comments by so many Balkars indicated, they continued to pray in their homes; the grandmothers continued to teach the grandchildren their religious heritage; and God continued to bless people, even in their times of distress.

318 Baysieva, interview.

In 1997 the Christian pastoral council of Kabardino-Balkaria made a decision to establish a Bible school to train pastors—the North Caucasus Bible Institute. Since that time, it has been training men and women for Christian service including preaching, teaching, counseling, media, worship, and mission work. It has since affiliated with the Moscow Theological Seminary of the Russian Baptist Union. The student enrollment grows each year, and students study in one of the nine academic programs, which include bachelor and master's level degrees. It is the only institution of higher theological education in the North Caucasus and during its existence has graduated thirty-five pastors; thirty-two teachers; five missionaries; and twenty worship leaders, preachers, and other lay ministers. Andrey Kravtsev has been the school's rector since 2004.

A faith or trust in God, aside from a religious label, runs deep in the hearts of the Balkars. As a famous philosopher from the ninth century BC, King Solomon, has written, God "has planted eternity in the human heart" (Eccl 3:11). Among the Balkars I met, each was convinced their survival and blessings indeed came from God.

22
Future Perspectives

Three major issues seem to top the list of concerns of the Balkars. The first is economic, and the desire for opportunity to thrive and improve one's lot in life. Unemployment, and the issues that go with it, continue to take a toll on the people themselves. Secondly, ethnic tensions with the Kabardinians are present, but seem to be decreasing in everyday life. There are intermarriages, collegial working conditions, and interethnic neighborhoods and villages. Finally, the violence brought about by Islamists is of concern to everyone. Most scholars, however, attribute this primarily to the lack of economic opportunities among the young.

The peoples of the North Caucasus republics are strongly identified with their own individual ethnic identities and do not see themselves as Russian in any sense of the word. Does this lead to more conflict with the central government of Moscow, or can ethnic identities survive peaceably with Russia? Some scholars believe that ethnic diversity can be tolerated both under a strong central government as well as in the absence or failure of state institutions. Some argue that animosity between the nationalities, ingrained from ancient times, is the motivating factor behind the current ethnic nationalism in Russia. However, it was in fact the Soviets' deliberate policies in the 1920s which fostered these strong ethnic identities. The affirmative action policy of the Soviet regime—creating boundaries, names, and languages for each people group—was intended to develop and promote the individual nationalities. Moreover, the deportation of entire population groups, including the Balkars, solidified each group's distinctiveness. Finally, combining returning deportees with unrelated ethnic groups within a single ethnic territory, presumably to weaken secessionist aspirations, was a deplorable policy, leading the way to the interethnic strife that threatens daily life in Kabardino-Balkaria and the other North Caucasus republics.

Arutiunov contends that "despite extensive ethnic diversity, the Caucasus region is not invariably condemned to ethnic turmoil."[319] While all of the nationalities pursue their cultural traditions and

> seek to establish ethnic "space," it would be misguided to assume that ethnic competition invariably leads to violent conflict. Only Chechnya has openly fought for full independence. Other strategies to increase ethnic autonomy include negotiating treaties with Moscow for new rights and privileges for

---

319 Arutiunov, "Ethnicity in the Caucasus."

the republic under the Federal Constitution (done in North Ossetia and Kabardino-Balkaria) . . . Even for groups fairly labelled as nations, the move to full independence may be undesirable, since none of the Caucasian republics can be economically self-supporting. The great mistake to be made in analysing the Caucasus is to assume that all groups are essentially nations seeking to carve out independent nation-states from the old Soviet republics.[320]

One can readily see that the western regions of the North Caucasus are more Westernized, with a greater majority of ethnic Russians, 80 percent, compared with the eastern regions of the North Caucasus, which only comprise 10 percent ethnic Russians. The level of industrialization and urbanization also declines as one moves east, just as the relative importance of the Islamic faith rises in the east.

In the KBR the population of nearly 1 million is only 10 percent Balkar, with Kabardinians at about 50 percent and Russians and other minority ethnicities at 40 percent. Relations between the Kabardinians and Russians are generally friendly; however, relations between the Balkars are more difficult, since they were subject to exile for thirteen years. Yet, Arutiunov notes that in spite of good relationships in many settings between the Kabardinians and Balkarians, "the social and political domination of the Kabardinians is a sticking point for many Balkars."[321]

Indeed the Balkars have called for an independent Balkar Republic in 1996 and in 2006, "but in both cases, Russian officials came down hard on them, and the movement appeared to dissipate. Now, however, the Balkars are again making demands." In March 2010, and again in August 2010, after a lengthy hunger strike in Moscow, the Balkars, "angered by what they see as the ethnocratic approach of the Kabard majority which dominates the Kabardino-Balkar Republic (KBR) . . . are again calling for the formation of a Balkar Republic within the Russian Federation."[322] Two goals of the hunger strike were to achieve local self-government and to deal with the land problems the highlander Balkars face. The land conflict is due to the lack of land for the villagers, and also the obstacles to shepherding in the highlands where the forests belong to the republic while the reserves belong to the federal government, making it difficult to get their cattle back between these properties without a passport. "As of today, not a single Balkar village has a hectare [approximately two and one-half acres] of land."[323]

---

320   Ibid.
321   Ibid.
322   Paul Goble, "Balkars Push for National Republic in North Caucasus," Eurasia Review, August 30, 2010, accessed July 13, 2011, http://www.eurasiareview.com/30082010-balkars-push-for-national-republic-in-north-caucasus.
323   Louisa Orazaeva, "Five of Moscow Balkar Hunger-strikers Hospitalized," Caucasian

So, in spite of the existence of many prerequisites of ethnic tension,

sober and balanced government leadership attempting to provide a decent niche for successful economic development may be able to prevent conflict. People who have some prospects of moderate economic success are not willing to sacrifice that prosperity to the selfish interest of nationalist politicians. Only where the hope for economic success is frustrated can such politicians have any sort of success.[324]

Arutiunov concludes that the conflicts are generally not ethnic, but rather economic, "triggered by the ongoing social and economic uncertainty, redistribution of property, [and] struggle for key positions."[325]

Contrary to perceived assumptions, the deportation and life in exile actually strengthened, rather than weakened, the national identity of the Caucasian peoples affected by them. The exile

revealed anew the importance of their "traditional institutions and national customs" and resuscitated stories of their distant past and national heroes, which tied them to their historic lands. Long after their return, the deportation remained—together with other formative components of their past—an integral ingredient of their ethnic identity.[326]

Russian policies continue to be haunted by the past, as 20 percent of the population of this country is considered minority, particularly Muslim, and the state is still seeking a way to deal with "porous borders" and the growing nationalism that was solidified by the deportation. With the Russian middle class currently at 15 percent of the population, and the rich at 1 percent, "much of the Russian citizenry remains mired in acute poverty: 12 percent have difficulty buying essential foodstuffs; 31 percent find it hard to purchase articles of basic clothing," and the situation among the Balkars is even more severe.[327] A survey conducted in 2006 found that "unemployment among young males in Russia's North Caucasus hovered around 30 percent (as compared with around 11 percent in the rest of Russia). In Kabardino-Balkaria, the figure was 35 percent."[328]

Since the disintegration of the Soviet Empire in the last century, the Caucasus region has experienced continual, serious disorder and degeneration.

Knot, August 12, 2010, accessed August 12, 2010, http://www.eng.kavkaz-uzel.ru/articles/14116/.

324   Arutiunov, "Ethnicity in the Caucasus."

325   Ibid.

326   Ro'i, "Transformation of Historiography," 168.

327   John Dunlop, "Russian Foreign Policy in the Twenty-first Century and the Shadow of the Past," *Slavic Review* 67, no. 2 (2008): 529.

328   Paxson, "Home," 34.

[Since 1991,] no part of the Caucasus has been free of armed conflict, economic deterioration, or political turmoil and confusion. As many as two million people have become refugees, tens of thousands have died. Food and medicines sent from abroad have kept hundreds of thousands of Caucasians from starving and dying of disease. These disasters have not happened because the Caucasus is a poor region. It is well endowed by nature. It has agricultural and mineral wealth, sufficient sources of energy to be a major exporter of oil. It has industries and potential for more industrial development. The peoples of the Caucasus are the heirs of ancient civilizations and high culture. They are literate, they are talented, and they are famous for their energy, ingenuity and skill as farmers, artisans, workers, and traders. Their professionals and intellectuals are the equal of any in the former Soviet Union.[329]

The nature of the Soviet/Russian system was so pernicious that it did nothing to prepare its colonies for independence as most other European colonial empires did.

The result of nearly seventy years of the Soviet system was that the most important human activities took place in the shadows, or underground. People depended on family, clan or colleagues from their ethnic group for support that enabled them to live some degree of normal life. The sense of civic responsibility that is necessary for the operation of modern societies atrophied. Peoples gained little experience governing themselves. "Socialist" government was seen as an enemy to be evaded, exploited, manipulated or cheated . . . All officials were regarded as dishonest and self-serving. No one was well prepared for the independence that suddenly came in 1991.[330]

As in the South Caucasus nations, the North Caucasus peoples simply had "little understanding of techniques of responsible governance of their own societies or experience in managing relations between countries and peoples."[331]

An analysis of differences of economic policies and structures related to economic performance showed that the primary difference was the presence of an industry or infrastructure which could support the economic growth of a region. The economic performance of the North Caucasus republics and the Kabardino-Balkar Republic in particular, is unstable and economically backward, and it is notable that there are no strong industries or infrastructure to support growth and economic improvement.[332]

---

329   Henze, "Russia and the Caucasus."
330   Ibid.
331   Henze, "American Interest."
332   Bert van Selm, "Economic Performance in Russia's Regions," *Europe-Asia Studies* 50, no. 4 (June 1998): 603–618.

Another argument regarding the stagnant nature of the Balkar economic situation relates to a larger conflict:

The prolonged conflict between the official Muslim hierarchy in the face of the republic's Muslim Spiritual Council and the so-called "new Muslims" ... the series of attacks in 2004 and 2005, the most prominent of which was the attack on October 13, 2005, on Kabardino-Balkaria's capital Nalchik, showed that the "Islamic question" has become the main socio-political problem in the republic.[333]

---

333   Sergei Markedonov, "The Plight of Kabardino-Balkaria," Circassian World, accessed July 15, 2011, http://www.circassianworld.com/new/headlines/1546-the-plight-of-kabardino-balkaria-by-sergei-markedonov.html.

23
Conclusion

There can be no question that the tiny nation of Balkarians has endured unspeakable hardships throughout their history. The deportation of 1944 was the most egregious of these, being imposed on the entire nation by a relentless, oppressive regime. Returning to their native homelands was something they had only dreamed of, without any hope that it might someday come to fruition.

However, this may not have brought the peace that the Balkars might have anticipated. Being assigned cohabitation with the Kabardinians has bred ongoing conflicts, jealousies, and injustices to the Balkars, including lack of self-government or participation in governing the republic; economic injustice; and a host of undesirable social ills, such as alcoholism, drugs, and violence.

However, their fierce commitment to their traditions and their stunning hospitality are the pervasive traits one encounters in individual Balkarians. They are indeed tolerant; they are genuine; they are ambitious, seeking higher education as a goal; they are hard-working as they eke out a living in the stark environment of the villages.

Though some commentators have purported that the younger generations are not embracing the long-held traditions of their ancestors, there is a deep awareness of those traditions. Like many young people, they are exposed to a new world and are testing the limits of their traditions. However, their inquisitiveness, their creativity, and their desire to please, combined with a continuing strong family structure, will ultimately draw them back to some form of traditions, not far from their parents.

Ruslan Vorovov, a third-generation descendent, says being in the Balkar community, the school, and the family, where everyone around him was raised in the traditions, has strengthened his character. He is very glad that he

> grew up here compared with other places in Russia. We are still holding on to moral standards that are good for society. It is part of our customs and traditions which help us live a life to respect elders and women. This community sets behavior standards and boundaries for behavior and that is positive.[334]

Kaplan Baysiev summed up the effects of the deportation saying:

-

---

334 Voronov, interview.

There were many tragedies, but it increased opportunities for our people. It was like a new page in the history of our people. It encouraged our minds, broadened our horizons. We saw a new type of life. People who never saw a train before were traveling on a train. We saw a big, wide world. It was difficult working in the mines, but it was an opportunity to earn a salary. My father had the opportunity to buy a car, which was one of the first cars in our village. So it was sorrowful, but increased the abilities, opportunities, and view of life.[335]

Marziyat Baysieva cites concern about the toll the deportation has taken on the people of her generation, noting with remorse the moral deterioration, the lack of concern for the elderly, and the selfish focus on their own lives.[336]

The idea that the current generation was losing some of their tradition was cited by many of the younger people, but in their hearts they were still trying to be Balkarian, as they understand it, in today's world. There are many problems in each generation, and the experiences and lessons of the former generations continue to inform the current generation as they seek peace and stability in their world.

335   K. Baysiev, interview.
336   Baysieva, interview.

Afterword

My last visit to the North Caucasus was in March 2011. Two weeks before I arrived, three people were murdered by terrorists very close to my destination in Kabardino-Balkaria. It was a political murder and another indication of the increased violence of the region. The villages were under a curfew with residents required to be off the streets by 9 p.m.; anyone entering the village after curfew was interrogated by the military patrolling the entrances. The local people were very concerned about their loss of freedom due to this terrorist action.

I was to be interviewed for the local Balkar newspaper, *Zaman.* I had been advised prior to the interview that I was not to mention anything about God or Christianity. My interviewer is also a person I interviewed for this book. I knew she was a Muslim, and she knew I was a Christian, but she wanted to keep that information out of her story for security reasons.

However, when she asked why I was writing this book and why I had even come to Kabardino-Balkaria, given the danger of the North Caucasus region, I faced a dilemma. How was I to answer this question without speaking of Christ? After consulting with my interpreter, and he with the interviewer, we all agreed I would answer according to my conscience. I told her that as a believer in Jesus Christ I had submitted my will to God's. I knew He had sent me to this place and that He had prompted me to write this book. I told her that I trusted Him to keep me safe, if that was His plan. But even if there were danger, I would rather encounter it as I obeyed God, rather than to disobey Him.

Then she asked, "What do you think the meaning of life is?" This is my answer that she printed in the Russian-language newspaper: "I am a believer in Jesus Christ, and for me the meaning of life is found in serving God. The Bible helps me find my way. Yes, you can do good deeds, even without faith, but without faith, I would not have a personal relationship with Jesus."

I do love the Balkar people, and I do sympathize with their history of terror and inhumanities. I really believe their story must be told. It is my hope that readers will pray for the peoples of the North Caucasus. I cannot help but trust that, as a result of writing this book, some of them will come to know Jesus as their Savior. That makes every danger worthwhile to me.

.

Glossary

8 March, 1944—The date of the Balkar deportation.

1917 Revolution—See October Revolution.

adat—Traditional Balkar law which regulates social and moral behavior; it has been passed on orally within families and the Balkar communities throughout the centuries.

affirmative action—Policies undertaken by the Soviets to give special consideration and benefits to certain people groups based on their ethnicity. (See *korenitzatsiia* and *natsionalizatsiia*.)

assimilation—The blending of ethnic minorities into the dominant society by using the dominant language and assuming the cultural ethics of the dominant society. Full assimilation occurs when new members of a society become indistinguishable from older/original members. In the Soviet Union, the term Russification was used interchangeably with assimilation, meaning to create Russians from the various ethnic peoples within the USSR, by using the Russian language, adopting Russian cultural elements, and eliminating the cultural traditions of these people as much as possible.

ayran—A traditional Balkar food which is thick, sour boiled milk mixed with water and salt, similar to yogurt.

Balkar holiday—Celebrated on 28 March, the Balkar holiday commemorates the Rebirth of the Balkar Nation after deportation.

Bolsheviks—The name of the Communist party which ruled from the overthrow of the Russian Empire in 1917 until the disintegration of the USSR in 1991.

bride-stealing—The practice of the groom "stealing" or "kidnapping" the young woman he intends to marry. It is commonly called "bridge-stealing," "bride-kidnapping," or simply "kidnapping." (See Chapter 3.)

Caucasian—The ethnic designation of individuals whose heritage is from the Caucasus Mountains.

Caucasus Mountains—The mountain range located in eastern Europe, in southern Russia, which goes across the isthmus between the Caspian Sea and the Black Sea. It contains the highest European peak, Mount Elbrus, which is located in the Kabardino-Balkaria Republic. Kavkaz is the abbreviated name of the Caucasus Mountains used by the people groups living in this region.

collectivism—The political/economic philosophy which places the group efforts over the individual efforts by combining the ownership of the means of production and collective decision-making within an organization or enterprise. In practice, in the USSR, it meant the government confiscating farms owned by individual families, and creating a large, government-run farm operation, using either hired or non-paid workers. *Sovkhozy* were government-run farms where the workers were hired; *kolkhozy* were government-run farms where the workers gave a percentage of the harvest to the government and were able to keep the remaining portions for their own families. (See *kolkhozy* and *sovkhozy*.)

deportation—The movement of people by the government in order to accomplish political or economic goals. The Soviets imposed "class-based" deportations on people within certain economic categories prior to 1933; from 1933 to 1953, deportations were carried out against people groups based solely on their ethnicity.

endogamy—Marriage within one's own social class. For example, the Balkars oppose marriage between Balkars and non-Balkars.

ethnic-based deportations—Deportations in the Soviet Union were originally based on economic class. From 1933 to 1953, deportations were based on ethnicity of the people deported and were carried out *en masse*, deporting all people of an ethnic group regardless of individual culpability.

ethnic cleansing—The forcible removal of an ethnically defined population from a given territory.

ethnic group—See people group.

ethnology—The study of various peoples and the differences and relationships among them, as well as the historical development of culture among peoples.

folk religion—A form of religion that does not necessarily adhere to standard doctrine and is based on the practices of a specific, usually local, people group. The peoples of the North Caucasus integrated aspects of the Muslim faith into their cultural traditions, rather than observing them as strictly religious.

genocide—The definition of genocide is used differently by governmental entities throughout the world and throughout history. The use of the term ranges from the extermination of an entire ethnic group of people to the establishment of circumstances that will not necessarily physically eliminate a people but will abolish their distinct ethnic identity. As examples, this can include forcing them to live in a more diverse ethnic environment, disallowing their cultural practices, and replacing their language.

glasnost—The policy of *glasnost* was introduced by USSR President Gorbachev, meaning "openness." In reality, this concept of "facilitation" enabled writers and journalists to claim a right to freedom of speech and publication. This was a joint policy initiative with *perestroika*. (See *perestroika*.) Together, these two policies led to the disintegration of the USSR and the resignation of Gorbachev in 1991.

Great Patriotic War—The name World War II was called in the USSR.

Great Purge—See Great Terror.

Great Terror—Also called the Great Purge, the period from 1935 to 1938 when individuals or groups who were charged with various crimes by the government were purged either by exile to labor camps (Gulag) or execution in the USSR.

Gulag—The Soviet system of forced labor camps used for criminals and political enemies.

hichini—The most famous, traditional Balkar food that is labor intensive, and is served looking like a stack of crepes with butter between the crepes.

Highlanders—The name commonly applied to the people who live in the Caucasus Mountains.

imam—A Muslim cleric.

jamaat—Assembly within the Islamic community. In the context of the North Caucasus, the *jamaat* is considered a community seeking to convert the political structure to Islamic sharia law by military or violent means. The *jamaats* seek young members, giving them a sense of community and belonging, and to train them.

Jewish deportations—There were two documented examples in the Old Testament of the capture and deportation of the Israelites to the conquering nations. Many of these Jews did not return to their homeland, and some of these are presumed to be the ancestors of Jewish people in the Caucasus Mountains. (See Chapter 11.)

jihad—There are three meanings of *jihad*. The first is the personal struggle to live the Muslim faith. Secondly, it is the struggle to build a Muslim society. The third use of this word gets the most attention, meaning a religious struggle, or war, to advance Islam and eliminate non-believers of Islam.

Kanokov, Arsen—The Kabardinian who was elected president of the Kabardino-Balkaria Republic in 2005 to the present.

Kavkaz—See Caucasus Mountains.

kefir—A traditional Balkar drink similar to liquid yogurt, kefir is milk that is fermented using grains.

Kokov, Valery—The Kabardinian elected as the first president of the Kabardino-Balkaria Republic from 1992 to 2005.

kolkhoz—(Plural: *kolkhozy*) Collective farms were created by confiscating land and combining small individual farms into a cooperative where the goods produced were shared among the workers based on the government-determined productivity of the farm, after giving a percentage to the government for redistribution. (See *sovkhoz*.)

Komsomol—Communist Youth League. The Komsomol had little direct influence on the Communist Party, but served as a mechanism to teach the values of the Communist Party to young people over the age of 14. It was considered an honor to be selected for the Komsomol, and awards and recognition were key components to motivating the youth.

korenitzatsiia—The Soviet policy of encouraging the ethnic groups within the North Caucasus to create their own nations, rather than assimilating the non-Russian peoples into the Russian ethnicity. This policy of nation-building was originally espoused by Stalin. (See *natsionalizatsiia*.)

kulak—An independent, relatively wealthy peasant who had increased his land holdings and was able to hire help with the farm. The *kulaks* were considered class enemies of the poorer farmers by the Communists.

Kurman—The celebration at the end of the Islamic thirty day fasting period of Ramadan.

Mountain Autonomous Soviet Socialist Republic—The Mountain ASSR was a short-lived republic in the Soviet Union from 1921 to 1924. It created districts, roughly corresponding to the current republics of the Balkars, Chechens, Kabardians, Karachay, Ingush, and North Ossetians. This Republic was replaced by the Stalin policy of *natsionalizatsiia*, which fostered the individual development of the people groups within the North Caucasus region, rather than treating all of the highlanders under one policy.

Mt. Elbrus—The highest mountain in Europe, located in Kabardino-Balkaria.

natsionalizatsiia—The original term for fostering pride in ethnic peoples within the North Caucasus, and encouraging their traditions, culture, and languages, to distinguish them from other people groups. Stalin used this term throughout his life, but the Communist Party expanded the term to *korenitzatsiia* to communicate a broader approach to the nation-building in the Caucasus. (See *korenitzatsiia*.)

North Caucasus Mountain region—Located in the southwestern portion of Russia between the Black Sea and the Caspian Sea, the region includes the Republics of Dagestan, Chechnya, Ingushetia, North Ossetia, Kabardino-Balkaria, Karachay-Cherkessia, and Adyghe.

October Revolution—Also called the 1917 Revolution, the October Revolution was actually a series of revolutions in the Russian Empire that culminated in 1917 when the Tsarist regime was overthrown and replaced by a Provisional Government, called the Russian Republic. Lasting only a few months, the Russian Republic was overthrown in October 1917 and replaced by the Bolshevik (Communist) government, which led to the creation of the Union of Soviet Socialist Republics (USSR), also called the Soviet Union.

Operation Deportation—The title used for the removal and relocation of several people groups within the Soviet Union. The practice ended in 1953, with the death of Josef Stalin.

pagan animists—"Pagan" generally refers to people who do not believe in a specific god, but rather practice as an animist, one who reveres spirits, particularly nature spirits and spirits of the dead.

people group—A group of people who are related ethnically, linguistically, culturally, traditionally, and geographically. This book uses people group, ethnic group, peoples, nation, and nationality interchangeably.

perestroika—A term popularized by USSR President Gorbachev which promoted restructuring politically and economically. In practical terms this meant the democratization of the Communist Party and the political system of the USSR. Economically, it legalized ownership of business ventures and liberalized price controls. This was a joint policy initiative with *glasnost*. (See *glasnost*.) Together, these two policies led to the disintegration of the USSR and the resignation of Gorbachev in 1991.

period of sadness—The Balkars observe a fifty-two day period of sadness when someone within the extended family dies. During this time, there are to be no celebrations, particularly weddings, out of respect to the deceased.

Piedmont Principle—This policy demonstrated conspicuous benevolence and special privileges toward the border nationalities within the Soviet Union, and in particular, the Caucasus region. It was intended to present and promote the superiority of the Soviet way of life to the neighboring countries across its borders.

Qur'an (Koran)—The holy book of Islam.

Red Army—The name used by the Bolshevik Army when it was fighting the anti-Bolshevik Army, called the White Army. The White Army was defeated in the October Revolution, and the Bolshevik, now Soviet, Army retained this title.

repatriation and rehabilitation—The name of the program granting permission to the deported peoples to return to their native homelands from their special settlements.

Russian Empire—The nation that existed from 1721 until 1917. It was ruled by an Emperor until 1905. Then it became a constitutional monarchy, ruled by Tsars. The Tsars were overthrown in 1917 and replaced by the Russian Republic, which lasted only a few months. The Bolsheviks overthrew the Russian Republic in October 1917 and renamed the nation the Union of Soviet Socialist Republics.

Sharia—Law of Islam which supersedes any political governmental law.

sovkhoz—(Plural *sovkhozy*) Government-operated farms created from confiscated lands of aristocrats. Workers, usually former peasants who did not own land, on the sovhoz were considered employees and were paid specific wages regardless of productivity of the farm. (See *kolkhoz*.)

special settlement—The places which were designated by the Soviets for the deported peoples to live. Usually they were barracks where many families lived together, but sometimes the people had to create their own shelters from sticks and dirt.

syncretism—The blending of various elements of different religions into one's own practice.

tawhid—The Islamic doctrine that confirms the oneness of Allah.

toponymy—The scientific study of place names to determine the origin of the words used.

Tsarist Empire—See Russian Empire.

Turkic peoples—Ethnic groups with an identity through language and customs to the Turkic peoples. Several of the North Caucasus inhabitants are linked to the Turkic peoples.

Union of Soviet Socialist Republics (USSR)—The USSR, also called the Soviet Union, was established with the overthrow of the Tsarist government in October 1917 by the Communist Party, the Bolsheviks. The Communist Party ruled the Soviet Union until it disintegrated in 1991.

xenophobia—The unfounded, irrational fear or suspicion of people of different ethnicities. The Soviet xenophobia was manifested in the exaggerated fear of foreign influence and foreign contamination of the Soviet methods. The Balkar xenophobia was manifested in the fear and antagonism to people outside their culture who might influence the practice of their traditions.

Bibliography

Arutiunov, S. A. "Ethnicity in the Caucasus: Ethnic Relations and Quasi-ethnic Conflicts." Circassian World. http://www.circassianworld.com/new/north-caucasus/1175-ethnic-conflicts-caucasus.html (accessed August 20, 2010).

Bachieva, Janna. Interview by author. March 16 and 24, 2011. Nalchik, Kabardino-Balkaria. Tape recording.

Balzer, Marjorie Mandelstam. "Nationalism, Interethnic Relations and Federalism: The Case of the Sakha Republic (Yakutia)." *Europe-Asia Studies* 48, no. 1 (January 1996): 101–21.

Bartles, Charles. "Russia's Islamic Threat: Book Review." *Military Review* 87, no. 6 (November–December 2007): 119–120.

Baysiev, Kaplan. Interview by author. March 17, 2011. Upper Balkaria, Kabardino-Balkaria. Tape recording.

Baysiev, Muhadin. Interview by the author. April 26, 2010. Upper Balkaria, Kabardino-Balkaria, transcript.

Baysieva, Marziyat. Interview by author. March 19, 2011. Nalchik, Kabardino-Balkaria. Tape recording.

Bullough, Oliver. *Let Our Fame Be Great.* New York: Basic Books, 2010.

Conquest, Robert. *The Nation Killers: The Soviet Deportation of Nationalities.* London: Macmillan, 1970.

Critchlow, James. *"Punished Peoples" of the Soviet Union: The Continuing Legacy of Stalin's Deportations.* New York: Human Rights Watch, 1991.

Dunlop, John. "Book Review: The Lone Wolf and the Bear: Three Centuries of Chechen Defiance of Russian Rule." *American Historical Review* 111, no. 5 (December 2006): 1636.

———. "Russian Foreign Policy in the Twenty-first Century and the Shadow of the Past." *Slavic Review* 67, no. 2 (2008): 528–29.

Eidelman, Tamara. "The Deportation of Peoples." *Russian Life* 52, no. 3 (May 2009): 21–22, 57.

Fuller, Liz. "Counterterror Restrictions Lifted in Kabardino-Balkaria as Insurgency Again Gathers Strength." Radio Free Europe / Radio Liberty. November 11, 2011. http://www.rferl.org/content/kabardino_balkaria_insurgency_north_caucasus_counterterrorism/24388125.html (accessed November 30, 2011).

———. "Kabardino-Balkaria Authorities at a Loss How to Cope with Militant Threat." Radio Free Europe / Radio Liberty. February 16, 2011. http://www.rferl.org/content/kabardino-balkaria_at_loss_on_militant_threat/2311663.html (accessed February 17, 2011).

———. "KBR President Condemns 'Genocide' of Balkars." Radio Free Europe / Radio Liberty, Circassian World. March 8, 2010. http://www.circassianworld. com/new/headlines/1446-kanokov-condemns-genocide-of-balkars.html (accessed July 16, 2011).

Gelastanov, Ibrahim. Interview by author. March 20, 2011. Nalchik, Kabardino-Balkaria. Tape recording.

Gerber, Theodore P., and Sarah E. Mendelson. "Casualty Sensitivity in a Post-Soviet Context: Russian Views of the Second Chechen War, 2001–2004." *Political Science Quarterly* 123, no. 1 (2001): 39–68.

Goble, Paul. "Balkars Push for National Republic in North Caucasus." Eurasia Review. August 30, 2010. http://www.eurasiareview.com/30082010-balkars-push-for-national-republic-in-north-caucasus (accessed July 13, 2011).

Griffin, Nicholas. *Caucasus: A Journey to the Land between Christianity and Islam.* Chicago: University of Chicago Press, 2001.

Gurtuev, Oyus. "Balkars' Hunger Strike in Moscow Lost Its Sense." Caucasian Knot. August 17, 2010. http://www.eng.kavkaz-uzel.ru/articles/14142/ (accessed August 18, 2010).

Hahn, Gordon M. "The Rise of Islamist Extremism in Kabardino-Balkariya." *Demokratizatsiya* 13, no. 4 (Fall 2005): 543–94.

Henze, Paul B. "American Interest in the Caucasus." Circassian World. http://www. circassianworld.com/new/north-caucasus/1167-american-interest-caucasus-henze.html (accessed July 15, 2011).

———. "Russia and the Caucasus." Circassian World. http://www.circassianworld. com/new/north-caucasus/1176-russia-and-the-caucasus-henze.html (accessed February 10, 2010).

Hirsch, Francine. *Empire of Nations.* New York: Cornell University Press, 2005.

Hunt, David. "Colour Symbolism in the Folk Literature of the Caucasus." *Folklore* 117 (December 2006): 329–38.

Huntington, Samuel P. "The Clash of Civilizations Revisited." *New Perspectives Quarterly* 24, no. 1 (Winter 2007): 53–59.

Karny, Yo'av. *Highlanders: A Journey to the Caucasus in Quest of Memory.* New York: Farrar, Straus & Giroux, 2000.

Kemper, Michael. "Book Review: Ethno-nationalism, Islam and the State in the Caucasus: Post-Soviet Disorder." *Journal of Islamic Studies* 19, no. 3 (2008): 423–26.

Khodarkovsky, Michael. "The Indigenous Elites and the Construction of Ethnic Identities in the North Caucasus." Circassian World. http:// www.circassianworld.com/new/north-caucasus/1169-indigenous-elites-khodarkovsky.html (accessed July 17, 2011).

King, Charles. *The Ghost of Freedom: A History of the Caucasus.* New York: Oxford University Press, 2008.

————, and Rajan Menon. "Prisoners of the Caucasus." *Foreign Affairs* 89, no. 4 (July–August 2010): 20–34.

Kolarz, Walter. *Russia and Her Colonies.* New York: Praeger, 1952.

Krag, Helen, and Lars Funch. "North Caucasus: The Region, the Republics and the Peoples." Circassian World. http://www.circassianworld.com/new/north-caucasus/1173-north-caucasus-region-people.html (accessed July 18, 2011).

Kulbaev, Alim. Interview by author several times during March 2011. Nalchik, Kabardino-Balkaria. Tape recording and transcript.

Kulbaeva, Svitlana. Interview by author. March 24, 2011. Nalchik, Kabardino-Balkaria. Tape recording.

Kulbaeva, Toma. Interview by author. March 20, 2011. Nalchik, Kabardino-Balkaria. Tape recording.

————. Interview by author. October 2, 2010. Moneta, Virginia. Transcript.

Kuliyev, Kaisyn. *Grass and Stone.* Moscow: Publishing Progress Publishers, 1977.

Malashenko, Alexei V. "Islam in Russia." *Social Research* 76, no. 1 (Spring 2009): 321–58.

Markedonov, Sergei. "The Plight of Kabardino-Balkaria." Circassian World. http://www.circassianworld.com/new/headlines/1546-the-plight-of-kabardino-balkaria-by-sergei-markedonov.html (accessed July 15, 2011).

Martin, Terry. *The Affirmative Action Empire: Nations and Nationalism in the Soviet Union, 1923–1939.* New York: Cornell University Press, 2001.

————. "The Origins of Soviet Ethnic Cleansing." *Journal of Modern History* 70 (December 1998): 813–67.

Metcalfe, Daniel. "Thorns in Russia's Side: *Let Our Fame Be Great* Book Review." *Spectator* (March 2010): 37.

Minahan, James. *Miniature Empires: A Historical Dictionary of the Newly Independent States.* Westport, CT: Greenwood Press, 1998.

Montefiore, Simon Sebag. *Stalin: The Court of the Red Tsar.* New York: Vintage Books, 2005.

————. *Young Stalin.* London: Weidenfeld & Nicolson, 2007.

Mukhina, Irina. "'The Forgotten History': Ethnic German Women in Soviet Exile, 1941–1955." *Europe-Asia Studies* 57, no. 5 (July 2005): 729–52.

Nekrich, Aleksandr M. *The Punished Peoples: The Deportation and Fate of Soviet Minorities at the End of the Second World War.* New York: Norton, 1978.

Olmezov, Usuf. Interview by author. March 23, 2011. Kashkhatau, Kabardino-Balkaria. Tape recording.

Orazaeva, Louisa. "Five of Moscow Balkar Hunger-strikers Hospitalized." *Caucasian Knot*. August 12, 2010. http://www.eng.kavkaz-uzel.ru/articles/14116/ (accessed August 12, 2010).

Paxson, Margaret. "They Call It Home." *Wilson Quarterly* (Spring 2009): 32–39.

Pohl, J. Otto. *Ethnic Cleansing in the USSR, 1937–1949*. Westport, CT: Greenwood Press, 1999.

————. "Stalin's Genocide against the 'Repressed Peoples.'" *Journal of Genocide Research* 2, no. 2 (2000): 267–93.

Ro'i, Yaacov. "The Transformation of Historiography on the 'Punished Peoples.'" *History and Memory* 21, no. 2 (Fall–Winter 2009): 150–76.

Schuessler, Jennifer. "Museum of Nations." *American Scholar* 70, no. 1 (Winter 2001): 145–48.

Shamanov, Ibragim, and Paul Friedrich. "Balkars." Encyclopedia.com. http://www.encyclopedia.com (accessed November 13, 2009).

Slater, Wendy. "An Ethnic History of Russia: Pre-revolutionary Times to the Present." *Journal of European Studies* 27, no. 4 (December 1997): 487–90.

Stepanov, Valery. "Ethnic Tensions and Separatism in Russia." *Journal of Ethnic and Migration Studies* 26, no. 2 (April 2000): 305–32.

Stern, Jessica E. "Moscow Meltdown: Can Russia Survive?" *International Security* 18, no. 4 (Spring 1994): 26–40.

Ulakov, Boris M. Interview by author. March 22, 2011. Köndelen, Kabardino-Balkaria. Tape recording and transcript.

Ulbasheva, Aishat. Interview by author. March 21, 2011. Yanikoi, Kabardino-Balkaria. Tape recording.

van Selm, Bert. "Economic Performance in Russia's Regions." *Europe-Asia Studies* 50, no. 4 (June 1998): 603–18.

Vatchagaev, Mairbek. "Rebel Attacks in Kabardino-Balkaria Skyrocket." *Eurasia Daily Monitor* 8, no. 25 (February 2011): 1–2.

Voronov, Ruslan. Interview by author. March 19, 2011. Yanikoi, Kabardino-Balkaria. Tape recording and transcript.

Warhola, James. "Religion and Politics under the Putin Administration: Accommodation and Confrontation within 'Managed Pluralism.'" *Journal of Church and State* 49, no. 1 (Winter 2007): 75–95.

Williams, Brian Glynn. "Hidden Ethnocide in the Soviet Muslim Borderlands." *Journal of Genocide Research* 4, no. 3 (2002): 357–73.

Zhanataeva, Madina. Interview by author. March 19, 2011. Nalchik, Kabardino-Balkaria. Tape recording.

Index